D0205022

Praises for Character First:

"If you're looking for a program, this isn't it. If you're searching for real change in your life and the people you live and work with, Character First is what you're looking for. Character awareness is all-encompassing. It's a small investment that continues to pay huge dividends."

> – **David Melvin,** President, David H. Melvin, Inc.

"One of our strategies for success is teamwork. 'If two or more agree on anything…it is bound by our Father in Heaven' (Matt. 18:19). But real teamwork is a rarity and only comes about with people who have a high level of trust. The Character First program has raised the level of trust of our employees which has led to the teamwork that helps make us successful."

> – **Joseph M. Oliver,** Chief Steward, Chairman and Founder Oliver Heating & Cooling

"Starting with our juvenile inmates, Character First has permeated the Oklahoma County Sheriff's Office. It is the avenue that changed the atmosphere where 2,400 inmates reside and 800 employees work. If we can do Character First here, it can be done anywhere."

> – **Argyl Dick,** chaplain to the Oklahoma County Sheriff's Office and Detention Center

"We found a way to import character into our world, and it hasn't been the same since."

—**Ken Krivanec**, Executive Vice President,
Quadrant Homes

"Character helps us build our ways of learning to learn…without that character, all the education in the world is meaningless."

—**Deborah Craven**, Counselor,
Crooked Oaks School

"We think Character First does what we want in terms of developing character for students."

—**Dr. James Branscum**, Superintendent,
Metro Technology Center

"All of our employees have undergone character training in the 49 areas that make up a business of character. We believe in building long-term relationships...that are founded on character."

—**Tom Gill**, Owner, Tom Gill Chevrolet

"The paradigm of Character First is that the right thing to do becomes the easiest thing to do."

—**Paul Mogabgab**, CEO, EDG, Inc.

"In the three years prior to our character initiative, we had 42 labor and employee grievances, and seven different lawsuits. In the three years since we put the character initiative in place, we have had two grievances and no lawsuits from employees. I think that, in and of itself, is significant."

—**Rodney Ray**, City Manager, Owasso, OK

MAKING CHARACTER FIRST

MAKING CHARACTER FIRST

BY TOM HILL

with Walter Jenkins

Character First Publishers, LLC
Oklahoma

MAKING CHARACTER FIRST
Copyright © 2010 By Tom Hill

First Edition

Hardcover:
ISBN: 978-0-983088-80-6
November 2010

Softcover:
ISBN: 978-0-983088-81-3

eBook:
ISBN: 978-0-983088-82-0

ePub:
ISBN: 978-0-983088-83-7

This publication is designed to provide accurate and authoritative information in regard to the subject matter covered. It is sold with the understanding that the publisher is not engaged in rendering legal, accounting, or other professional service. If legal advice or other expert assistance is required, the services of a competent professional person should be sought.

From a Declaration of Principles jointly Adopted by a Committee of the American Bar Association and a Committee of Publishers and Associations

1. Business 2. Leadership 3. Management 4. Organizational Change 5. Strategic Planning 6. Ethics

I. Hill, Tom II. Title

Making Character First may be purchased at special quantity discounts to use as corporate premiums, sales promotions, corporate training programs, gifts, fund raising, book clubs, or educational purposes for schools and universities. For more information contact Robert Greenlaw at Character First, 13800 Benson Rd, Suite 206, Edmond, OK 73013, 877-357-0001 or email us at: info@characterfirst.com.

To reach people around the globe in their own language, we have a rights and licensing department. For translation or reprint rights in English or any other language in book or electronic format contact Mel Cohen, 1000 Pearl Road Pleasantville, TN 37033, 931-593-2484 or email Mel at melcohen@hughes.net.

Character First is a registered trademark of Character Training Institute
www.characterfirst.com

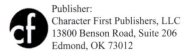

Publisher:
Character First Publishers, LLC
13800 Benson Road, Suite 206
Edmond, OK 73012

Cover design: Tom Hill, Thomas Hill, Lynne Hopwood

Design: Lynne Hopwood

This book is dedicated to the memory
of my friend, father-in law, and mentor,
Garman O. Kimmell

1913 – 2008

The Hill Family

ACKNOWLEDGEMENTS

To say this book was written by Tom Hill is an oversimplification. Without the patient, loving encouragement and help of my wife, it would not have been written. She is the love of my life and my partner of 47 years. She has helped inspire whatever good character I have. She has been a co-writer, editor, creative director, and counselor. Most of all, she has continued to love me through it all.

My children and grandchildren have also been an integral part of this book. Not that they are all writers or editors, but they have been a great encouragement as my character continues to be transformed. I am especially grateful for our two daughters-in-law and our son-in-law; who with our children have given us 20 grandchildren. They are the delight of our lives and in many ways our "character classroom."

And finally, I am grateful to God. He loves me in an incredible and indescribable way, gives meaning and purpose to my life, and gives me the strength to "walk the talk" on those occasions when I do.

Contents

Foreword

I met Tom Hill years ago and have been fascinated ever since by his family's business, Kimray Inc., and the culture of character they have been so successful in developing. At Yale University, we have gone so far as to make Kimray a case study to teach students about good management.

In addition, this year I took a close look at Kimray for a PBS documentary called "Doing Virtuous Business." This Emmy-nominated program spotlights several inspirational business success stories. In addition to Tom Hill, many of the world's most influential entrepreneurs and chief executives are featured, representing well-known companies such as Dannon, ServiceMaster, Four Seasons, Wal-Mart, Tyson Foods, Herman Miller, Cargill, Habitat for Humanity, Cummins Engine, and Chick-fil-A Restaurants.

Kimray and the other organizations in the documentary have developed what can be called a "values-based" management strategy. In doing so, they found they can improve not only their bottom line, but also the company's relationships—with customers, employees, vendors, the environment, and the world at large.

Tom Hill and the Kimray team were leading with this type of strategy long before it became popular. What's more, by focusing on character, they discovered principles that apply to organizations of all sizes, in all cultures. As a result, the impact of their Character First program has spread around the world—and continues to grow.

Today, Kimray is a great company making a positive difference for its shareholders, employees, customers, vendors, and the community in which it operates. But that wasn't always the case.

Kimray is what we refer to as a "turnaround." This book explains how Tom led that turnaround and how Kimray's unique character-building program transformed the corporate culture. It empowered a faltering company not just to survive, but to thrive.

I don't know what Tom's character was like when he initiated the turnaround. But I can tell you that today, Tom is wise about good character—because he has it, and because he has helped to nurture it in so many other people, companies, and civic organizations.

Kimray is but one sound example of how character can build, nurture, and transform a culture. Their example provides a model from which other companies and organizations can learn. This book provides useful forms and processes that can benefit all companies, everywhere.

The notion of character may seem old-fashioned or passé in a world where decadence, triviality, and debauchery abound. Nothing could be further from the truth, as this simple yet powerful book by Tom Hill attests. Character is about conscience, doing the right things, nurturing good habits, and building the virtues of individuals and teams. In this business model, character dictates noble purpose, and purpose paves the way for success.

Leaders play a critical role in character building. They inspire it and exhibit it. They recognize it and praise it. They do so often and constantly. This process, which is never ending, is not a quick fix or a fad-of-the-month. When practiced studiously, it makes for a highly effective organization.

In the end, you can't force change. Rules and dictates won't do it. But leaders can lead change. People are emotional, physical, and spiritual beings who can be inspired. In fact, they are made with a desire for success. They want to be virtuous. How do you start down this virtuous path? Build character first.

Try it! It works. It is also a right, honorable, and good thing to do.

Theodore Roosevelt Malloch, Ph.D.
Chairman and CEO, The Roosevelt Group
Research Professor, Yale University

Introduction

"Because it is the right thing to do!"

During the last five years, I have been privileged to witness Newell Rubbermaid flourish. It is based on a very unique culture or value system based on Character First.

Business is not only about making money, although unarguably it is the most necessary objective. Without profitability, there will be little credibility left in terms of how we manage our resources. However, sharing the same call of profitability in every business, how can we run it differently—in a way that is holistic, meaningful, sustainable, and with great passion?

Many businesses share the common challenges of maximizing earnings, reducing costs, improving quality and services, beating the competitions, etc. However, at the bottom of all these, none can deny it is the people who make all these things happen—or fail to happen.

Although I agree that top talent is important to the success of the business, I also believe that the best-run businesses today that have sustainable profitability over a long period of time are those which are able to unleash the potential of all their individual employees, no matter how "average" they are. And this unleashing of their common employees' potential is not about their muscles and minds—it is all about their hearts.

Character-building goes right down into individuals' hearts. It is about changing our attitude, our will, and then our behaviors and our habits. It is about building a holistic relationship with co-workers, customers, suppliers, and all business associates, with the same standard of moral excellence everywhere and all the time. Character is about freedom to choose to do the right thing and to do it right. Character is also a life-long journey.

Character unites all the employees together with the same standard of values, behavior, aspiration, and thus builds strong associates relationships. It creates a powerful culture to propel everyone to lead with excellence, dedication, and passion. When we focus on doing the right thing because it is right, we never have to worry about the day-to-day results; because somehow, the right values determine the right response, and the right response will align with the right processes, and the right processes give rise to the right results, and then the right results collectively give rise to above average profitability continuously.

Finally, character building is the most powerful form of leadership influence. Character establishes leadership by moral authority and not just by power and position. While power and position alone will enforce outward compliance, only leadership that is based on character that is manifested through day-to-day life will truly engage inside-out voluntary commitment and dedication and frees up true creativity and innovation, both at the individual as well as the corporate level.

Tai Chau Chyi
Vice President Operations
Newell Rubbermaid
Shanghai, China

PROLOGUE

For Thomas, running a company is more than his job. He loves what he does, he loves the people, and he loves his product and the service he provides. He pours his life into his work, goes to sleep thinking about it, and wakes up with it on his mind. His job is his passion, the air that he breathes, the blood in his veins. He gives it more hours and thought than anything else—sometimes to the detriment of his family.

In spite of all that Thomas does, things don't go as planned. There are problems, some with solutions but others that overwhelm him. So he works more hours, spends more time thinking about work, and dedicates more of himself to it. He tries to run the company on the sheer power of his will. He has a few minor victories, but, more often than not, he wonders how he is going to navigate through the challenges.

The others in the company are important, but he doesn't believe they share his passion or commitment. He feels as if they walk out the door at five and don't think about the job until eight the next morning. They return to work and pick up where they left off the night before. He comes to work hours ahead of them in terms of thought and planning.

Most of his employees are hardworking, but a few come to work late, aren't 100% attentive while at work, or fail to even show up. Most are loyal, but several turn against him and talk about his failures behind his back. Others question his motives and his character. This small percentage of employees demands the majority of his attention. He feels alone and isolated. He thinks, "I've worked long hours and made personal sacrifices to provide my employees with jobs and make them successful." Now he wonders, "Why?" It is a bitter pill to swallow.

That was the story of my first 20 years at Kimray. If you have been the leader of a team or company—or if you have ever had the joy and privilege of pouring your life, heart, and soul into something you love—you probably understand the frustration I experienced.

Much of my leadership in the early years focused more on myself than on my employees. Looking back, I realize that many of my actions were more about my pride and my desire to succeed rather than the welfare of my employees. I thought I could force success by working longer hours and sacrificing for those around me. That is a proven recipe for disaster, and I lived it every day for two decades.

The Character Solution

But the story doesn't end here. There is a way to lead your team to greatness. There is hope, and there can be a light at the end of the tunnel that isn't a train. The problems we face are frequently *personal character issues* that cannot be solved with programs, techniques, or more hours at the office. Creating a culture of character within our organization is the solution to many of these challenges. Fortunately, there is a way to make this transformation that has been tried and proven in a myriad of arenas.

There are many definitions of *character*, including being an *odd person*. But character as defined in this book is not personality or reputation but moral constitution. It is what drives a person's attitudes, words, and actions.

Be forewarned. Character is a leadership issue. The success of transforming the culture of your company is directly related to your ability to recognize and repair your own character deficiencies. Character begins at the top. However, your personal character is not the only issue. You must be committed to teaching and modeling good character to others.

This book begins after my first 20 years at Kimray and contains the "turnaround" story of the next 20 years. By applying the message of this book, you can avoid some of the grief I experienced from self-absorbed leadership. When you focus on the success of your employees and co-workers, creativity is released, responsibility is seized, and dependability becomes commonplace.

CHAPTER 1

REFLECTIONS

I park my car in front of the main offices at Kimray and gaze into the clear, blue Oklahoma sky. A spring breeze ruffles the blooming flowers, neatly trimmed trees, and shrubs framing our manicured lawn. I take a few moments and reminisce.

Main Offices and Plant

Kimray manufactures and distributes valves and controls for the oil and gas industry. My father-in-law, Garman Kimmell (1913-2008), founded the company on August 31, 1948. He was my mentor and friend for 45 years, my boss for 37 years, and will always be my hero.

A brilliant design engineer and committed Christian, Garman had resigned from Black, Sivalls & Bryson in May of 1948 after declining to move his family from Oklahoma City to Kansas City. His employment contract gave his former employer the rights to any of his new inventions for the next three years. With monetary and managerial assistance from his father, Garman O. Kimmell, Sr., he acquired the rights to the design of a back-pressure valve.

Old and New Valves

After redesigning it, Kimray began producing a three-inch version. Originally peddled out of the back of a pickup truck, it is still a staple of Kimray's current product line, made essentially the same as in 1948. The durability and simplicity of the valve provided income for Kimray to expand their product line, which eventually would include 30 of Garman's patents on regulators, pumps, and gas measurement.

Kimray has grown from two employees to over 550; from a few hundred square feet in an old renovated grocery store to 400,000 in the Santa Fe Industrial area of Oklahoma City; and from one distributor to 30 distributors spread across 15 countries. Our company-owned distributors, and those operated by independent contractors, serve virtually every oil and gas field around the globe.

Original Store

Today, our family's third generation is managing Kimray. One of my sons serves as the CEO and the other as the President. It is difficult for any family-owned company to survive three generations, and we are blessed to have successfully transitioned to this point. Both of my sons lead Kimray with the values and character that their grandfather instilled as the founder. He would be pleased to watch them enthusiastically guide the business with a commitment to integrity.

Kimray Building 1955

The Shop

I walk into my office and glance at my desk, the cabinet behind it, and the framed pictures on the walls. My office has

Three Generations, 2004

remained virtually unchanged over the past four decades. The only major difference since my semi-retirement is that my desk is nearly clear of paper and projects. It was never clean when I was working full time.

The muffled hum of machines floats in from the shop. This sound has been such a part of my life that most of the time I don't notice it. But at the start of each day, it's a reminder to me of where the value is created for Kimray customers. I walk out of my quiet office, put on a pair of safety glasses, and enter the machine shop at Kimray. I have walked through this shop thousands of times, and it is still a thrill. I love the sight of hundreds of men and women working in harmony, the hum of the machines, the smell of lubricating oil, and the bins filled with parts and finished products. For most of my adult life, my clothes have been saturated with the aroma of this shop and the soles of my shoes embedded with oil and tiny pieces of metal.

A drill press sits on a workbench to my right. Gray metal shavings pile up around the tip of a spinning drill bit. An employee on the other side of the shop bangs a hammer, and the sound echoes off the walls. In the distance, a forklift scurries between workstations, and the driver beeps his horn as he approaches each corner.

To many people these noises would be an unpleasant distraction, but to me they are melodious. The sounds reassure me that hundreds of employees are working together to complete our common goal.

On my left, men take raw castings, place them into horizontal lathes, and then remove them after the Computer Numerically Controlled (CNC) machines turn the dull metal into precise, shiny parts. Our engineers set standards requiring that the finished products meet those measurements within thousandths of an inch. We won't ship anything that falls outside of these tolerances.

Computer Numerically Controlled (CNC) Machines

I pass underneath one of the red and gray banners that hang overhead and read its message, "Under-promise, over-deliver."

On my right sits a high-speed, computer-controlled transfer machine. It feeds castings through three separate milling heads. As the castings pass through each stage, the computer software determines which tool is needed and automatically selects the proper one from an enclosed rack.

Another forklift whizzes past me, and the driver smiles and nods as he honks his horn. I take a breath, and the smell of oil is replaced with fumes from the machines. Many of our cutting tools are cooled with a water-based lubricant. It has an unmistakable and comforting smell, like our kitchen after my wife's bread has come out of the oven.

Even after all these years, I cannot help but marvel at the frenzy of the machine shop. To the untrained eye, a manufacturing plant looks chaotic and disorganized. Nothing could be further from the truth. Nothing happens on the manufacturing floor that hasn't been thought about long in advance, and every move has purpose and direction. There is no wasted energy.

A successful manufacturing plant is one of the most complicated organizations in the world. Each worker has a specific job that must be done in a precise way and at a precise time. Anyone who gets even slightly out of step will cause a bottleneck that impacts not only the employee and that department, but also the entire company. If one part is delayed in the manufacturing process, products cannot be completed on time and shipments are delayed. This means delayed payment and lost opportunity from future sales. Customers have options, and if their products are not delivered on time, they may never buy from you again. However, the worst part of not delivering products on time is that a commitment to a customer has been broken.

I sometimes compare a well-run machine shop to a high-performance racecar. When all of the parts are working together, the car races along the track, lap after lap. But if even the smallest part fails or one member of the pit crew makes a mistake, the car could malfunction, resulting in disaster. It takes an entire team to win the race.

I walk deeper into the plant and look at our inventory, a huge wall of raw castings stored on large shelves behind gray, mesh wire. Eventually, all of this will be machined, painted, assembled, and delivered to a customer.

Warehouse

Even ordering inventory is complicated in a manufacturing facility. We purchase, manufacture, and inventory over 10,000 different parts. Castings and raw materials are ordered months in advance based on our expectations of future orders. We use our experience, market conditions, and gut instinct to determine what products to manufacture at what time. We may also get an unexpected call tomorrow from a customer wanting a specific part, and this adds complexity to the equation.

Powerful high-speed milling machines line the far south wall of the machine shop. Within them, "tombstone" fixtures nearly two feet tall and weighing hundreds of pounds hold the parts being machined. The internal milling heads move back and forth with such force the machines have to be bolted to the floor or they would slide across the room, like giant out-of-balance washing machines.

High-speed Milling Machines

I turn the corner, and a machinist steps toward me. "How are you?" he asks.

"Great." We smile and shake hands. You can tell a lot by a person's hands. In his, I instantly feel the years he has spent at Kimray. We have chatted many times on the shop floor. Looking him in the eyes, I am reminded that people built Kimray. They are the true value of this, or any, company. Machines are important, but the people are the heart, soul, mind, and spirit of any organization.

He also reminds me of the sense of family we have at Kimray. His nephew works nearby in our shop, and that's not unusual. There are several families with three or even four members working for us. We are proud that so many of our employees refer friends and family when they know we have an opening.

I walk to the paint booth and watch an employee paint a batch of machined castings that are suspended by chains traveling along an inverted track. The painter spins the castings, and as they whirl round and round, he aims his pneumatic paint gun and pulls the trigger. The parts emerge bright red and are shuffled further down the track to dry.

Paint Booth

Kimray red has become more than just a color. It is a bond that joins our employees to our customers. When our customers see Kimray red, they know the care and quality that has gone into each part, and they expect years of reliability and value. When our employees assemble or ship Kimray red parts, they know how privileged we are to serve our loyal customers. The diligence and determination our employees put into each and every item we ship help make Kimray a great company.

I wind between the machines and head for the door that leads to my office. I look back at the machine shop and smile. It's easy to smile now. We are profitable, we have dependable, committed employees who work with character, our deliveries are on time, and many of our customers are raving fans. Kimray has distinguished itself as doing business in a principled and ethical manner. This hasn't always been the case. It wasn't long ago that we questioned every aspect of how we were doing business.

I take off the safety glasses and sit in the black mesh chair behind my desk. It's quiet. I already miss the sounds and smells of the machine shop.

CHAPTER 2

SEEDS OF OPPORTUNITY

It was January 1963, and I was driving my 1955 Buick Special to pick up a girl for a blind date that had been arranged by a friend. Following the directions he gave me to her house, I pulled into the driveway behind a middle-aged gentleman who was unloading boxes from the back of his car. "Need some help?" I asked.

"Sure."

Picking up the first box, I noticed the Kimray name on it. My stepfather had been a machinist at Kimray for the last four years. I asked the man, "Do you work for Kimray?"

"Well—sort of. I'm the President."

That should have been my clue to get in my car, back out of the driveway, and return to my parents' home. I was a 19-year-old who had flunked out of high school, joined the Marines, and was now stationed in Grand Prairie, Texas. I had come to the city for the weekend to visit family and friends. This girl was clearly out of my league.

But Marines aren't easily intimidated, so I finished carrying boxes into his shop and proceeded to take his daughter on the date. As it turned out, meeting Garman Kimmell and his daughter Kay are two of the greatest blessings of my life.

Kay and I were married that July. Later that same year, I was commissioned as a Marine Warrant Officer and trained as a Radar Intercept Operator to fly in the back seat of F4-Phantom jets. I spent seven years in the Marine Corps, including a one-year tour of duty in Vietnam during 1965-66.

VMFA 323 Vietnam 1966

In December 1967 I resigned from the Corps and moved Kay and our two boys from Brunswick, Georgia, to Stillwater, Oklahoma. After a few false starts choosing a college major, a battery of aptitude tests directed me to electrical engineering.

During the summers, I worked for Mr. Kimmell on various projects and odd jobs for his home and company, trying to earn enough money to put food on the table while going to college on the G.I. Bill. Mr. Kimmell had three daughters and no son. My own father had been killed in a car-train wreck three weeks before I was born; therefore, it was easy for me to develop a very close relationship with him. Even so, I knew and worked for him for six years before I ever addressed him in any way other than "Mr. Kimmell."

An Exciting Start

A few months before my graduation in May of 1971, Garman offered me a job as an applications engineer at Kimray. Without the slightest hesitation, I accepted. My entire life up to that point had been spent in school or the military, and I was excited about the opportunity to enter the business world.

The 1970s were interesting times for any oil-related company, because there was a worldwide shortage of oil. Gasoline was in short supply, and there were long lines at the gas pumps. People waited in their cars for hours for the chance to buy gas.

Exploration for new sources of oil and gas was at an all-time high; consequently, so was the demand for our products. Our sales projections were based solely on our manufacturing capacity. If we could make it, we knew we could sell it. We didn't worry about adding sales staff to our rapidly growing company—customers came to us. Kimray expanded from 64 employees with $4.5 million in sales in 1971 to 285 employees with $30 million in sales in 1981.

Oil and Gas Tank Battery

Such rapid growth in the oil industry created a lack of knowledgeable and experienced employees. There were so many new oil wells being drilled around the country that there weren't enough qualified people to work all of them. In response to this need, I was assigned to travel around the oilfields and train people to properly install and operate our products. I dealt mostly with oilfield workers, which was a great opportunity for me to learn firsthand the oil and gas business—but I didn't learn much about leading people.

Several of Kimray's top management retired in 1977 after serving Kimray for almost 30 years. Garman was a first-class engineer and inventor, but he had little desire to run the company on a day-to-day basis. However, his vision was for the company to continue to be family-owned and operated, and so one day he called me into his office.

Garman told me that my time in the Marines, followed by the maturing process of marriage, parenting, working, and being mentored by him for eight years had developed my character along with my experience. He asked if I would step in as Executive Vice-President. He was confident that with our close association, he could provide the experience and wisdom I lacked. I readily accepted his offer. I forged ahead with great passion, enthusiasm, and determination. Unfortunately, those qualities, as good as they are, cannot replace experience.

The vast majority of the people who have worked for Kimray have been people of great character who gave an honest day's work each and every day. But as our revenues and number of employees grew, so did our problems. I didn't take the time to watch what was happening with our employees. It wasn't denial, but I was blind to seeing the way new hires were changing our company.

"One bad apple spoils the barrel," an old proverb says. A few employees hired over the course of months can destroy the

Tom and Nancy Rice, Kimray's HR Manager, 1977

heart and soul of a company that has been carefully cultivated for years. Sometimes, however, you don't know you have bad apples. If you don't lift the lid off the barrel occasionally and smell an apple going bad, you never know it's there. Over a period of time, it became obvious we had a few bad apples— new employees with bad attitudes and actions.

Peeking into the Apple Barrel

One morning I noticed a long line of employees standing outside the superintendent's office. After the line was gone, I asked the superintendent about the problem. He told me, "These employees were late. They have to explain why they weren't here on time and get my approval before they can clock in and start work."

I was dumbfounded. "That's what tardy students had to do in high school. They had to get a hall pass before they could go to class." These were adults, not students. Why were so many arriving late and others failing to show up?

The superintendent also told me if he didn't accept the reason an employee gave for being late, or if an employee was habitually late, he would either send the employee home without pay or fire the employee. It occurred to me these punishments hurt the company as much as the employee. Fewer employees meant fewer hours worked, fewer products manufactured, and lower profits.

Another morning, I was in my office early when my phone rang. An irate woman on the other end of the line started screaming at me. Her husband, one of our night-shift workers, had just come home from work. He was high on drugs he had purchased from a friend and used at Kimray, and this was not the first time it had happened. I soon learned a few of our employees were smuggling drugs into work in their lunchboxes and radios. We quickly made rules that allowed us to administer drug tests. If an employee failed one, he was fired.

Some time later, a friend told me he was at a flea market and saw someone selling small, portable air tanks equipped with Kimray pressure gauges. We had not sold them for that application, so there was only one explanation—they had been stolen. After investigation, we discovered one of our supervisors had been taking parts and entire valves, slipping them out the back door, and recovering them when his shift was over. He then sold them illegally to the highest bidder.

The lid was off the apple barrel.

CHAPTER 3

BAD APPLES AND RULES

It was exciting to become Executive Vice-President of Kimray, and I looked forward to the challenges and rewards of leadership. But as the problems swirled around me, it became extremely stressful and draining. I relied on my training as a Marine and hoped to solve the problems with swift and decisive action. Under my directive, each time we saw a wrong behavior, we reacted by creating a new rule designed to prohibit that behavior. The consequences for violating rules grew tougher and tougher.

No Standing on Toilets

I was looking through our book of ever-increasing rules one day and read a rule I did not understand and could hardly believe. *You will be fired for standing on a toilet seat.* I thought, "That's an actual rule?" I read it again to make sure it wasn't just my imagination.

I asked our plant superintendent to explain. "It's a good rule, and we have to have it," he said.

Some of our bad apples were going to the toilet, sitting down, and falling asleep. A supervisor would eventually notice someone missing and start looking for the employee. The search would lead to the bathroom where the supervisor would discover feet under the walls of the stall. After checking several times and seeing no movement, it became apparent the employee was asleep. So a new rule was enacted: "No sleeping on the toilet." But our bad apples were creative in avoiding work. (If only they had shown so much initiative and determination to complete the tasks they had been hired to perform!)

They would still sleep in the bathroom but to avoid detection, they would sit on the water tank on the back of the toilet with their feet resting on the toilet seat. This behavior gave birth to another rule, "No standing on the toilet seat." Who would ever imagine we would have to make a rule prohibiting an employee from standing on a toilet?

A Crazy Cycle

We thought we could prevent problems by making rules to forbid undesirable behavior. It soon dawned on us that rules didn't stop problems. They only caused our bad apples to find more and more creative ways to circumvent the rules. We were locked into an ongoing cycle of discovering problems, creating rules to solve the problems, waiting for the bad apples to find a way around the rules, and then creating more rules.

We were spending more time creating and enforcing rules than solving manufacturing and delivery problems, and we had plenty of those. We had a 42-week lead-time for the delivery of new orders. This failure to promptly deliver product had opened the door to five new competitors who manufactured similar, if not identical, products.

As we were trying to return our focus to the manufacturing and delivery side of the business, our personnel manager brought another problem to our attention. A small group of bad apples regularly ate lunch together and returned to the plant with cups full of soda mixed with alcohol. One of them was a lead person, and she made job assignments based on whom she liked. Her friends got the prized jobs, while the rest of the workers were assigned less desirable tasks. We investigated the situation, called them in, and fired them. But the problem did not end there. Despite the evidence we had to prove what had happened, we were sued for defamation of character. (The lawsuit was later dropped.)

I couldn't believe what had happened to Kimray. We started out as a great company with great employees, but our productivity and morale had fallen to an all-time low, our workers' compensation costs were at an all-time high, and our profit margins were slim or non-existent despite the fact we had raised our prices four times in four years.

Picking Bad Apples

The oil and gas business is never stable for very long. It consists of a series of very intense "boom or bust" cycles. The boom cycles can last anywhere from two to 10 years. During the boom times, unemployment in the entire region is low, and it becomes challenging to hire good employees.

By 1979, the unemployment rate in Oklahoma was about 3.5 percent. It was extremely difficult—if not impossible— to find, hire, and retain workers. We took whatever new hires we could find and did everything possible to retain the employees we had. We tried conventional ways to hire employees by advertising in the newspaper, working with employment agencies, and posting openings on the plant bulletin boards.

We received very few applications using these methods and scoured them to see if they listed any experience in a machine shop or manufacturing plant. We reviewed their *training and education. Although we requested references, we were thrilled to have any potential new hires, even if we weren't always able to verify their complete work history.*

What became obvious as time passed, however, was that some of the new employees had changed the culture of the company. I had contributed to the change by failing to provide leadership and not communicating our core values. A few bad apples created hardships for our good employees, and, over the course of several years, destroyed the culture of character it had taken Kimray decades to build. We needed a way to return to the culture that had made our company great.

CHAPTER 4

WISDOM

The problems at Kimray seemed to grow by the day and began to look insurmountable. I lamented to a friend about the challenges we faced and what we had done to try to resolve them. He made an observation that radically changed my outlook as a leader.

We were addressing each issue as a separate problem, and for each problem we created a new rule with strong penalties for violating it. As I thought about this, I remembered our growing rulebook and prohibition against standing on toilets.

Rules are enacted to change the employees' environment—or scare them with the fear of punishment—in the hope of changing their behavior. By doing this, we were addressing the surface issues and not the root causes. We were treating the symptoms but not the disease. All of our problems, although they looked different, had a common root cause—a lack of good character. The solution was to address the problems, not as separate issues, but as different manifestations of the lack of character.

An illustration of this concept is a fruit tree. It bears fruit according to its kind. An orange tree produces oranges, and an apple tree produces apples. No matter what you do, you cannot get oranges from an apple tree. We were falsely expecting good fruit from individuals with poor character.

> *A tree is known by its fruit; A man by his deeds.* Saint Basil

Bad character produces bad fruit—bad attitudes, words, and actions.

Examples of Bad Fruit

*The fruit of **confusion** is **disorganization**.*

*The fruit of **rejection** is **anger and bitterness**.*

*The fruit of **deception** is **stealing**.*

*The fruit of **inconsistency** is **low productivity**.*

*The fruit of **resistance** is **personal agenda**.*

*The fruit of **tardiness** is **poor attendance**.*

*The fruit of **unreliability** is **negligence**.*

*The fruit of **unawareness** is **avoidable accidents**.*

*The fruit of **self-indulgence** is **alcoholism** and **drug abuse**.*

*The fruit of **covetousness** is **ungratefulness**.*

*The fruit of **unconcern** is **poor quality**.*

All of the negative behaviors we had endured, the rotten fruit, had been caused by the same root problem—poor character. We had tried to fix these issues by prohibiting bad fruit (making rules), not realizing that we would never reap good fruit until we addressed the issue of character.

BAD FRUIT

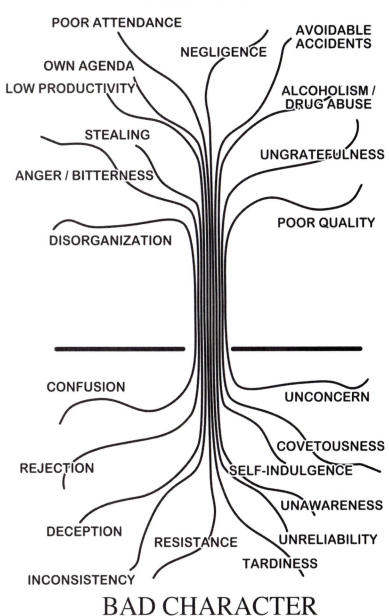

BAD CHARACTER

The solution to all these problems would be to encourage the development of good character in our employees. We would know we were successful if the fruit were different. If we developed a root system of good character, the fruit would be good attitudes, words, and actions.

Examples of Good Fruit

*The fruit of **orderliness** is being **organized**.*

*The fruit of **forgiveness** is **bearing no grudge**.*

*The fruit of **truthfulness** is **being trustworthy**.*

*The fruit of **dependability** is high **productivity**.*

*The fruit of **flexibility** is **team players**.*

*The fruit of **punctuality** is **good attendance**.*

*The fruit of **responsibility** is **reliability**.*

*The fruit of **alertness** is **fewer accidents**.*

*The fruit of **self-control** is **freedom from substance abuse**.*

*The fruit of **contentment** is **gratefulness**.*

*The fruit of **attentiveness** is **quality work**.*

Emphasizing character would result in less reliance on rules and rule keepers and allow our supervisors to focus on manufacturing issues instead of personnel problems. We named this new paradigm of corporate training "Character

GOOD FRUIT

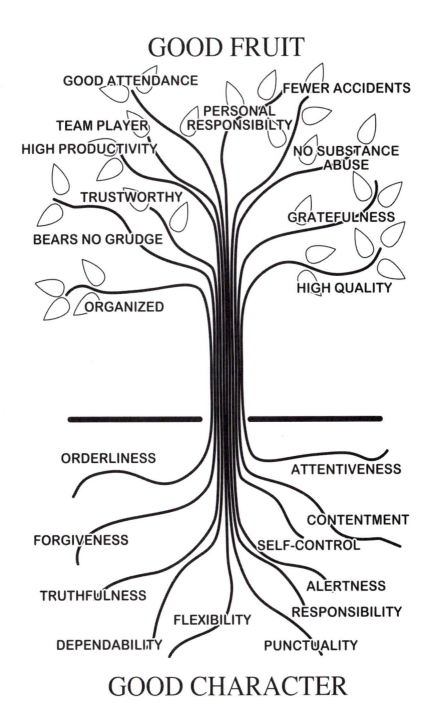

GOOD ATTENDANCE

FEWER ACCIDENTS

PERSONAL RESPONSIBILTY

TEAM PLAYER

HIGH PRODUCTIVITY

NO SUBSTANCE ABUSE

TRUSTWORTHY

GRATEFULNESS

BEARS NO GRUDGE

ORGANIZED

HIGH QUALITY

ORDERLINESS

ATTENTIVENESS

CONTENTMENT

FORGIVENESS

SELF-CONTROL

TRUTHFULNESS

ALERTNESS

RESPONSIBILITY

FLEXIBILITY

DEPENDABILITY

PUNCTUALITY

GOOD CHARACTER

First." We have been using Character First at Kimray for nearly two decades, and the results have been dramatic.

For example, after only two years we cut our workers' compensation costs by 80 percent. We thought this might have been an anomaly, but another company later applied Character First and experienced a 90 percent drop in its workers' compensation rates in two years.[1]

How can emphasizing character reduce workers' compensation costs? Many people believe most work-related accidents are the result of poor workplace conditions. If someone is hurt on the job, they assume there was a slick spot on the floor or a machine that malfunctioned. That may have been the case in the past, but it is less common today. Every company wants to keep on-the-job accidents to a minimum, and many studies have been done to determine why workplace injuries happen so that they can be eliminated. The results may surprise you.

Shortly after we experienced the decline in workers' compensation costs, I received a letter from the insurance company HRH (now known as Willis HRH), stating that only six percent of workers' compensation costs are caused by workplace conditions. Two percent are the result of uncontrolled events generally called "acts of God." The remaining 92 percent of all workers' compensation costs can be directly attributed to employee negligence, fraudulent claims, and inflated claims.[2]

During the following months, I noticed more and more articles dealing with workplace accidents. An *Industry News* article stated 80 percent of all injuries are caused by people—not by workplace conditions. A study by The Wyatt Company (a global consulting firm now known as Towers Watson) found 30 percent of hospital admissions for workers' compensation injuries to be unnecessary. Still another study indicated 80 percent of all hospital bills are incorrect, and two-thirds of these reflect overcharging.[3]

An article on controlling insurance costs stated, "Mechanical problems such as defective wiring, poorly designed and maintained machinery, and inoperative emergency equipment, are only a minimal part of a company's loss exposure. Human error counts for nearly half of all fire losses and 90 percent of industrial accidents."[4]

According to all these reports, the average company could eliminate 80 to 90 percent of work-related accidents and workers' compensation costs if it could eliminate negligence, fraud, human error, and inflated claims.

Each of these issues can be traced to poor character. Negligence is the result of not being alert, attentive, or cautious. It also shows that we are not being obedient and following the appropriate rules and procedures. Fraud is another word for not being sincere and truthful. Human error can be reduced when we are more alert to our surroundings and more attentive to instructions and safety rules. Inflated claims are the result of not being truthful in reporting either the extent of the injuries or where the injuries occurred. They also show that we are not accepting responsibility for our actions.

As our workers' compensations costs plummeted, our personnel problems also dropped, while morale and productivity soared. For several years, Kimray experienced record profits and had an on-time delivery rate of over 90 percent. Our customers noticed a positive change in the interactions they had with our employees. Several asked us what we were doing differently, and we eventually started training companies so that they could implement Character First.

Over the last four years, we have grown an average of 25 percent per year. The Greater Oklahoma City Chamber named us a "Metro 50" winner for four consecutive years, recognizing us as one of the area's fastest-growing privately-owned companies. Several of those years Kimray was the only manufacturing firm on the list and was the only company that has been in business for over 60 years.

Kimray has been named to the list of "Best Places to Work" and has received the "Compass Award" from the Oklahoma Ethics Consortium. We now have over 500 employees, and our revenues exceed $150 million a year.

Character First is not the only reason Kimray has grown, but it has helped us foster a culture of character where employees can grow and contribute to the success of the company, their families, and their communities. This has allowed our company to expand at an unparalleled rate. Our managers can solve manufacturing and delivery issues instead of spending excessive amounts of time on personnel matters. It has truly repaired our culture and made the company great again.

CHAPTER 5

WHAT IS CHARACTER?

The key to restoring the culture at Kimray was to begin teaching good character. Before turning this concept into reality, three serious questions needed to be answered:

- What is character?
- Can you build or change your character or the character of others?
- If you can build or change character, how do you do it?

Let's start with the first question.

What Character Is *Not*

People are often confused about character. Perhaps the best starting point is to say what character is not.

It's Not Reputation

Thomas Paine, one of America's founding fathers, said it best: "Reputation is what men and women think of us; character is what God and the angels know of us."

The less you know about a person, the more you rely on his or her reputation—the public image you perceive whether reading about him, seeing her on TV, hearing him speak, or listening to reports from other people. The more you know about a person, the more intertwined his or her character and reputation become.

Because of my work, I am fortunate to meet many people. If they have heard or read about me before I am introduced, their concept of me is my reputation, but they really do not know my character. They are relying solely on what they have heard about me.

Employees at Kimray have a closer view of my character. They see me regularly and have watched me respond to different situations. My reputation with them may be closer to my actual character.

To my children, my reputation and character have become well interwoven. But to my wife, my character has completely meshed with my reputation. We have been blessed with nearly 50 years of marriage. My reputation and character are synonymous to her because she knows me so intimately.

It's Not Personality

Personality has more to do with natural traits of behavior. My wife and I see this vividly portrayed in our 20 grandchildren. Each of them has a different, unique personality. No two are alike. Some of them like to sing when they play, while others are silent. Some of them are very outgoing and have never met a stranger, while others are more reserved.

All personality types can display good character. For example, the shy grandchild can still be hospitable and bold. She can have good character even when some character traits are different from her personality.

It's Not Religion

Many people define character in religious terms, but a person can have any religion or no religion and still have character. I have had the privilege of speaking in over a dozen foreign countries to people of different religions, including Buddhists, Christians, Jews, and Muslims. My experience is that all religions hold character in high esteem. Some of them place more emphasis on character than others, but all appreciate good character and define it as what they consider "moral" or "upright."

So Then What Is Character?

Character is an inner sense of right and wrong with a commitment to do what is right regardless of the cost. When confronted with choices that have moral consequences, good character is what guides me to make the right decision.

Character First Key Term
Character: *An inner sense of right and wrong with a commitment to do what is right regardless of the cost.*

> *Of all the properties which belong to honorable men, not one is so highly prized as that of character.* Henry Clay

Internal Navigation System

It takes a lot of time and training to be part of a high-performance aircraft crew. When I first began flying in an F4-B Phantom jet with the Marines, we were only allowed to fly VFR (Visual Flight Rules) during daylight and clear weather. Flying into clouds or at night is very dangerous for pilots, because there are no reference points, and they quickly lose their bearings. They must reject their natural senses and trust the aircraft's instruments. Much of our training was devoted to giving us the confidence we needed to understand and rely on our instruments.

There are two primary instruments that help pilots keep their bearings regardless of the circumstances outside of the plane or what their senses tell them. One is a compass. It tells the pilot which direction a plane is headed, whether it is north, south, east, or west. The other is the attitude indicator. It tells the pilot whether the nose of the aircraft is pointed up or down, as well as whether the plane is banking left or right.

A pilot's senses may tell her the plane is headed one way, but she has to look at her compass and attitude indicator to know with certainty. Only then can she safely reach her destination.

Our character is the same. When we build good character into our lives, circumstances may indicate doing one thing, but our inner compass tells us, "No. That is not the right thing to do." Good character is always good character, regardless of the choices we face.

A man's character is his fate. Heraclitus

Internal Plumb Bob

Another character analogy is a plumb bob, a string with a pointed weight on the end. Bricklayers, masons, and carpenters have used this instrument since the time of the ancient Egyptians to make sure their projects were "plumb," or perfectly upright. Good character is like a plumb bob, telling us when our actions are "upright."

Good character—like a compass, attitude indicator, or plumb bob—is an absolute that will guide you in the right direction regardless of circumstances.

A Little Voice

We all have a conscience. Our character is driven by our conscience. Part of good character is developing a strong conscience and understanding how to listen to it when making decisions. When confronted with a choice, there is a process that happens in my head. It is as if one voice says, "Go ahead. It is only a small thing. Do it. You will enjoy it."

Then another voice says, "No. Don't do that. It is not right." Consistently doing the right things—even in small matters—develops a strong conscience that encourages good character.

> *Character may be manifested in the great*
> *moments, but it is made in the small ones.*
> Phillip Brooks

You can warp your conscience by doing the wrong thing so often that in your mind it becomes the right thing. Eventually, our conscience will stop speaking to us if we consistently ignore its warnings. That is why it is so important to be reminded of what good character is. Only then can we make the right choices, even regarding little things.

Qualities Built into Your Life

Character First uses a more formal definition of character: "The qualities built into an individual's life that determine his or her response, regardless of circumstances."

The true test of character is our response to morally or ethically challenging questions during difficult times, when we think no one will ever know what we do.

> *The measure of a man's character*
> *is what he would do if he knew he would*
> *never be found out.*
> Baron Thomas Babington Macauley

I was explaining this concept during a seminar in Beijing, China, "A person's character is like a tube of tooth paste. You don't know what is inside until you squeeze it."

A man in the audience added, "We have a saying in China: 'You can't tell how strong the tea is until you put the tea bag in hot water.'" We may have been from two different cultures on opposite sides of the planet, but we were of one mind when it came to character.

> *Good character dictates right attitudes,*
> *right words, and right actions,*
> *not just when it is easy*
> *but in very difficult situations.*

CHAPTER 6

CAN YOU BUILD OR CHANGE CHARACTER?

Once we defined character, we had to address whether or not it was possible to build or change character, in yourself and in others. There seem to be three prevailing viewpoints on this.

Some people think you are born with a certain amount of character and this is all you will ever have. It is a trait, like your eye color or whether or not you have a cleft chin. You will never have more or less character. You can't add to it. You can't change it.

Other people say that the majority of your character is developed as a child. According to this theory, by the time you are 10 or 12 your character is cultivated and set for the rest of your life. You won't be able to appreciably add to or subtract from it after that. It seems to be a twist on the old proverb, "You can't teach an old dog new tricks."

Most of us inherently know that these two ideas are wrong. We have seen in our own lives and in the lives of those around us that character can be changed. Many of us know someone who was making poor character choices but then began making better choices and lived a better life.

For instance, one goal of incarcerating people who commit a crime is to rehabilitate them—to change their character. If we believed criminals couldn't change, we would lock them up forever—even after a first offense. But we don't do that. We give people the opportunity to change their character, because we know they can.

I am an example of a person who changed his character. Early in my life, I regularly made poor character choices and did the wrong things, even though I knew better. Few people who know me now would ever suspect this.

Once I started being around more positive character influences, my life changed forever. My attitudes, actions, and words improved, and I took steps that benefitted my life and the lives of those around me. I know people can change their character, because I did it. And if I can do it, so can others.

> *He who walks with the wise grows wise,*
> *but a companion of fools suffers harm.*
> Proverbs 13:20

A Little Help from My Friends

One of the reasons I was able to change my life was because of people who mentored me. A mentor takes a genuine interest in someone else, teaches him or her how to make good decisions, and holds him or her accountable. There is an increasing interest in mentoring today. Advocates of mentoring have statistics that show when people are mentored, they have a much greater chance of being successful in life, because good mentors teach and model good character.

> *Associate yourself with men of good quality*
> *if you esteem your own reputation; for 'tis*
> *better to be alone than in bad company.*
> George Washington

Several powerful mentors blessed my life. One was my father-in-law. It was a privilege watching him model good character and learning from him for 45 years. I developed an immense amount of respect for him and wanted to be like him. When making decisions, I would ask, "What would Garman do?" This guided my character development.

For example, I had been a smoker since my early teens. I had quit smoking several times but always started again. As Mark Twain said, "Giving up smoking is the easiest thing in the world. I know because I've done it thousands of times."

One of the reasons it was so hard to quit was that many of my co-workers were smokers, including Garman. As soon as I quit, I would see someone at work with a cigarette and succumb to temptation.

One day during my late twenties, I noticed Garman wasn't carrying his usual pack of cigarettes. "I quit," he told me. "I realized that every time you quit smoking and came to work with me, you started smoking again. Now that I have quit, Tom, you have no excuse."

I took my cigarettes out of my pocket and put them on the dresser. I never had to quit again. Once my father-in-law had kicked the habit, I knew I could, too. That is how powerful a mentoring relationship can be. His example helped me break my addiction.

Daily Choices

We are all constantly building our character. The only question is, "Are we building good character or bad character?" We build good character by doing the right thing, even regarding the smallest decisions. This reinforces our conscience—our inner sense of right and wrong. As a result, we condition ourselves to respond with good character when the tough times come.

> *Character is the by-product; it is produced*
> *in the great manufacture of daily duty.*
> Woodrow T. Wilson

To change our character, we must acknowledge that our character (words, actions, and attitudes) has been wrong. We must take personal responsibility for the consequences of our bad character. Then we must purpose to change.

Some people say we have no individual responsibility for our actions, we have no free will, and our actions are driven by our circumstances. This false concept promotes irresponsible behavior and a victim mentality. Until we accept personal responsibility for our actions and their consequences, there will be no change for the better—only more and more bad character.

Changing our character also requires a change in our mindset. Some people think that the little daily decisions don't really matter. They believe they can avoid acting with good character in certain situations, especially when it involves something small. They believe that when they get into a serious situation and are required to make a *big* decision, they will respond correctly. Unfortunately, history teaches us adversity doesn't build character. It only reveals the character we have already built.

> *We imagine we would be all right if a big*
> *crisis arose, but the crisis will only reveal*
> *the stuff we are made of. It will not put*
> *anything into us... Crisis always reveals*
> *character.* Oswald Chambers

So we need to prepare for adversity by doing the right thing and building character before we face tough situations. That way, when we must make a difficult decision, we will have the best chance of making the correct one. We won't even have to think about it. It will come naturally.

There is a wonderful little poem that reminds me of this:

> *Sow a thought, and you reap an act;*
> *Sow an act, and you reap a habit;*
> *Sow a habit, and you reap a character;*
> *Sow a character, and you reap a destiny.*
> Unknown

Build a strong conscience so that you will have the right thoughts, even regarding small things. This will build your character and eventually your destiny.

CHAPTER 7

THE REAL QUESTION

That left us with the final question, "How do we build character in ourselves and our team?"

I have spent several decades talking with people around the world about character. My experiences have made me sure of one thing. I cannot build character into your life, and you cannot build character into my life. I can encourage you, but I can't make decisions or changes for you. I cannot force you to develop good character. You can continue to make bad choices in spite of what I do.

What I can do is instill a desire in others to develop good character. Nothing will change until they take action. So the real question is, *"How do we inspire the members of our team to change their character?"*

Different from Building Skills

It is important to understand the differences between how we build character and how we build skills. Teaching character the same way you teach skills is ineffective. A skill is a learned activity. Reading, riding a bike, operating a machine, playing a piano, and competing in sports are all skills. Skills can build on each other. Learning one skill can pave the way to learning another one.

Gaps in Time

Once you become proficient, no one can take a skill away from you. You may be more or less talented than other people, and you may need to practice to perform at a higher level, but once you learn a skill it is yours. For instance, if you learned to ride a bicycle as a child, you can probably ride today if your health allows, even if you have not ridden in many years.

When he was 12 years old, our son David spent several months learning to ride a short unicycle. Once he became proficient, he desperately wanted my wife and me to buy him a tall unicycle. Only a few people have ever tried (much less mastered) riding a tall unicycle, so we made a deal. "We'll pay for the unicycle," we told him, "but for every day it takes you to learn to ride, you have to pay us a dollar, up to half of the cost."

The day we brought the six-foot unicycle home, David leaned it against our neighbor's house, climbed aboard, and took off. The tall unicycle didn't cost him one dollar! David is now in his forties, married, and has a family. He seldom rides his unicycle. But whenever he wants, David can climb on his tall unicycle and pedal around the block.

Failure

The role of failure is different when learning a skill than when building character. Failure can be a profitable—and often necessary—part of learning a new skill. You make mistakes and hopefully learn from them. It is not how many times you fall down. It is how many times you get back up. You don't really fail until you quit trying.

> *Character consists of what you do on the third and fourth try.* James A. Michener

What happens when you fail in character? Character is really about relationships. It's about how people interact and the behaviors we expect from one another. Consequently, a character failure almost always fractures a relationship. The results can be devastating, and *you may never* get an opportunity to restore the relationship.

This is especially true when poor character violates a person's trust. Trust is a character issue. To be trustworthy, people have to demonstrate many character qualities, including loyalty, truthfulness, and sincerity. It takes a long time to rebuild trust once it is damaged, and *you may never* enjoy the same level of trust again.

A Chinese proverb says, "Trust is like a piece of fine china. If you break it, it can be fixed. But it will never be quite the same again." We can do the right thing for years and years, but one bad character decision can damage our known character and our relationships with people we care about. We can repair it, but the process can take a long time, and the relationships may never be the same.

> *Character is much easier kept than recovered.* Thomas Paine

Of course, the permanent damage from character failures can extend well beyond our personal relationships. People who commit a felony must face their character failure every time they try to find a new job, even long after they have changed their character and stopped committing crimes. When they fill out a job application, they will have to answer "Yes" when asked if they have any felony convictions, unless they receive a pardon. That is an extreme example, but it shows how character decisions may shadow you for a lifetime. Bad decisions can be difficult, if not impossible, to overcome.

Incentives

A person can be motivated and encouraged to learn a skill with monetary incentives, grades, or rewards. For example, you may be paid to receive training for a new job, which could result in a higher salary and a promotion. The pay and the potential of advancement might motivate you to attend class, apply yourself, and master new skills.

Paying someone to build character is usually not effective. For instance, imagine that one of your employees is consistently late. You call him into your office and inform him you cannot promote him or give him a pay raise because he is not punctual. But suppose you offer him an incentive and say, "If you will come to work on time for two weeks, I will promote you and give you a raise."

What do you think will happen? Most people will say, "He will show up on time for the next two weeks, gladly take the promotion and higher pay, and quickly revert back to his old habits." Why do we expect him to act this way? Because it is human nature. We intrinsically understand you can't inspire people to change their character with the promise of raises, rewards, or promotions. You have to use different methods to get long-term results.

Rewards can be a part of character training, but they should be unexpected and infrequent. Rewards do not always motivate good character. In fact, they can have the opposite effect if not used properly.

Let's look at an example. Suppose I take my four-year old grandson to the store. He whines, cries, and fusses so much it embarrasses me and distracts all the other shoppers. I lean down and tell my grandson, "If you will be good, we'll get an ice cream cone when we leave."

What will my grandson do? He will probably settle down because he wants the ice cream. We leave and, true to my promise, we get some ice cream. The situation is resolved—at least temporarily. What just happened? My grandson was rewarded for displaying bad behavior. He was trained to get a treat by throwing a tantrum.

What would be better? I should take my grandson aside, talk to him about his behavior, and calm him down. If the remainder of our shopping trip was peaceful, I might say as we leave the store, "You were obedient and demonstrated self-control in the store. As a treat, we are going to get an ice cream cone." Do you notice the difference? This is the first time my grandson has heard about the reward. It is a surprise and unexpected. The lesson he learned is that he may be rewarded for obedience and self-control, but if he is disobedient he will receive nothing.

To be effective, rewards should be unexpected and infrequent. If my grandson received an ice cream cone after every trip to the store, it would become expected and lose its value as an unexpected reward for displaying good character.

My grandchildren are often in plays, piano recitals, and ball games. We frequently go for ice cream after a game or performance is over, and they sometimes even ask, "Are we going for ice cream?" In this instance, the ice cream is not a reward for good behavior. It is acknowledgement for learning and demonstrating a skill. It's similar to getting an "A" on their report card.

If rewards don't inspire good character, what does? One of the best ways to inspire good character is to look for good behavior and recognize or praise it.

CHAPTER 8

THE POWER OF PRAISE

Everyone has an intrinsic desire to please authority figures, especially those they respect. An employee wants to please her boss. A child wants to please his parents. A student wants to please her teacher. Even if they don't realize it, people like to make their superiors happy.

Our need to please creates another desire. We need to know when we have pleased our supervisor, parents, or teachers. But how do we know when we have their approval? We know when our behavior is recognized and praised. Everyone, consciously or subconsciously, is looking for recognition and praise from the authority figures in his or her life.

What is praise? Many people would define praise as "when someone says something good about me." We frequently associate praise with a compliment. Unfortunately, people are generally praised insincerely, for achievement, or as a means of manipulation.

In the context of character training, praise has a much narrower definition. Praise is pointing out words, actions, and attitudes that demonstrate character qualities and explaining how they benefit you and those around you.

> **Character First Key Term**
> **Praise:** *pointing out words, actions, and attitudes that demonstrate character qualities and explaining how they benefit you and those around you.*

A New Mindset

Most people and organizations praise for achievement. However, as Character First has demonstrated, when you begin praising for character, you can change the culture of your organization. When we praise employees for the character they demonstrate and tell them why it is important, it gives them a roadmap on how to succeed. It encourages them to base decisions on character and inspires them to develop good character. Unfortunately, most managers do not know how to praise for character. Why is this?

Managers are trained to find problems and fix them. Our livelihood often depends on our ability to find what is wrong and make it right. Unfortunately, this often prevents us from seeing the good a person does.

> *If you feel constrained to look for mistakes,*
> *use a mirror not a telescope.* Unknown

I have a knack. I can walk into our plant, look at a thousand machined parts piled in a basket, and pick up the only defective one in the batch. I naturally ask, "Why is this part bad?" It would be better to say, "Wow! There are 999 good parts here."

We tend to treat people the same way. It is easier to see their mistakes and correct them than to see what they are doing properly. Managers often think, "I've told them a hundred times what to do. Why aren't they doing it?"

We "expect" people to do the right thing, and when they meet our expectations we see no reason to praise them. We only notice the times they don't meet our expectations. Therefore, we often seem to be telling them what they did wrong and correcting them. Our motivation may be to help them improve or to improve quality, but the unintended consequence is that they become discouraged and quit trying.

> *Don't wait until people do things exactly*
> *right before you praise them.*
> Ken Blanchard

There is a saying, "People join companies, but they leave bosses." Studies show the number one reason people leave organizations is *limited recognition and praise.* More people quit for this reason than because of compensation.[5] When we are always correcting and seldom praising, employees can get discouraged and begin to think, "There is no way I can ever please my supervisor." People don't want to work where they only hear about their mistakes.

Looking for Character

Looking for good character and praising it was a new concept for me. As a manager, my job was to find and resolve problems, not give out compliments. When I did praise an employee, it was usually for achievement, not character.

I began to understand that praising for character could change the culture at Kimray. This was going to be a difficult transition, so I couldn't afford to send any mixed signals. If we said character is important, but primarily recognized and rewarded achievement—even indirectly—it would have prevented us from making any real change. If my employees (or my children) believed achievement was what mattered, they might be tempted to do whatever was necessary to produce achievement. Every decision needed to be based on character.

When Do You Praise for Character?

I knew we could praise individuals daily in the course of normal activities in conversations, in written notes, or by email. We could also praise for character when we celebrated successes and special events. In addition, we decided to implement employee meetings where the supervisor would praise employees publicly on their anniversary with the company. In each case we would identify a character quality that the employee regularly exhibited, define the character quality, give an example of how the employee demonstrated that character quality with actions, and tell the benefits.

How does this inspire character? First, the manager learns to look for the good character of an individual, rather than focusing on the negative. Second, the good character that was exhibited is reinforced. The employee learns what the supervisor appreciates and why it is beneficial. In addition, everyone hearing the praise learns about the character quality and its benefits. They hear examples of how that character quality was displayed in the workplace. Furthermore, a common language of character is developed within the organization.

Praising Character Rather Than Achievement

How does praising character differ from praising achievement? Let's look at an example. Suppose a manager overhears an employee talking to an irate customer. Maybe a delivery was missed or the wrong product sent. The employee is patient, doesn't get upset, and works with the customer to resolve the problem. The conversation ends with the customer satisfied that the situation will be corrected.

Suppose the manager told the employee, "Good job. I'm glad you were able to handle that upset customer. We need the sales volume." That would be praising for achievement. The focus is on the end result, not the character.

How can we praise for character rather than achievement? Praise is pointing out words, actions, and attitudes that demonstrate good character and explaining how they benefit you and or others. Using the above example, the manager might say, "I appreciate your patience in dealing with that customer. Patience is accepting a difficult situation without giving a deadline to remove it. You took the time to properly resolve a very difficult situation. That was a good example to me. It reminds me it is better to keep an existing customer than to find a new one."

In the latter example, the manager praised the employee for the character quality of patience, not for the results. Our natural tendency is to praise for achievement. We don't naturally look for and praise character. We have to learn how to do it. Learning how to praise for character begins with looking for words, actions, and attitudes that deserve praise. *Look for the good in others and praise it.*

Flattery and Manipulation

The concept of praising for character is not universally understood. Some feel that all praise is flattery or a means of manipulation. My wife and I were in Malaysia at the International Conference on Families and Children. We spoke to a large assembly of delegates from many nations on, "True Success: Becoming a Family of Character."

When we were finished, a mother approached us with a question. "If you praise your children, won't they become proud?" Yes, children could develop a negative pride, but that generally occurs when the praise is 1) for achievement, or 2) insincere and undeserved.

Another Chinese proverb says, "If you want to get even with a man, flatter his children." An ancient adage tells us, "Flattery spreads a net for the feet." Both recognize and speak to the fact that flattery, insincere praise, and praise only for achievement are destructive. But praising for character inspires a person to build more character.

Why? Being a man or woman of character is not a competition where one person wins and another loses. One person having character does not prevent another person from having character. In fact, the ideal is that we would all have good character.

This is the major difference between Character First and Employee of the Month (EOM) programs. In EOM programs, one employee is selected at the exclusion of all others. But other employees know that the EOM's accomplishments required their help to some degree or another. He or she didn't earn the reward single-handedly—it took teamwork, and everyone had to work together to achieve a common goal. When we select one employee as the EOM, it tends to destroy team spirit.

The goal of Character First is to encourage all employees to reach their full potential by developing good character. In our employee meetings, we select employees to praise on an impartial basis, such as their anniversary date with the company. Over the course of the year, every employee will be publically praised.

This is not like some children's team sports, where there are no winners or losers and everyone gets a trophy at the end of the season. The employees should not be praised just for "participating," but for demonstrating character on a daily basis.

Daily Praise

Recognizing and praising a person for character is not something that you only do occasionally. The real impact happens when we recognize and praise for character on a daily basis. In *The One Minute Manager*, Ken Blanchard wrote that instead of looking for the bad in our employees, we should "catch them doing something right" and praise them for it.[6] It's easy to miss the importance of this.

Two Stanford University professors conducted an interesting experiment. They divided workers into two groups. The first group worked with computers that were programmed to offer occasional words of praise, while the second (control) group received no electronic encouragement. In addition, the professors told the first group the words of praise meant nothing because they had programmed the computers to deliver random praise.

The first group, even after they were told the guidelines of the experiment, *still* reacted positively to the praise. They stated they felt a greater sense of working as partners than those on the other machines. As a result, they worked longer hours, got more pleasure out of tasks, and felt more confident about trying new things.[7]

If random praise from a computer makes employees feel better about themselves and their work, how much more would sincere praise from their boss affect them? Never undervalue the importance of daily praise.

Paul Cook, CEO of Raychem Corporation, explained the importance of praise. "The most important factor is individual recognition—more important than salaries, bonuses, or promotions. And their greatest reward is receiving acknowledgement that they did contribute to making something wonderful happen."

Saying "good job" or "nice work" doesn't do the job. Instead, recognize employees by praising for character and communicating appreciation. Let them know they are vital to the organization and encourage them to continue building their character.

Once we begin looking for character qualities to praise at the monthly meeting, it becomes more natural for us to recognize good character and praise it every day. Praising character daily helps break the cycle of only correcting our employees when they do something wrong. It allows us to walk by the parts bin and see the 999 good parts, not just the one bad part. (Note: The bad does need to be corrected. See chapter 18.)

Praising for character inspires and encourages others to build character in their lives. It properly recognizes people for demonstrating good character. It teaches what good character is and establishes a "language" of character in an organization. Praising for character tells an employee what a manager appreciates and also communicates to others how they can demonstrate good character. It helps cultivate good relationships. Praising for character is a simple, but powerful, way to help others be successful.

> *A child is molded by the praise of his parents.*
>
> *A man is molded by the praise of his wife.*
>
> *An employee is molded by the praise of his boss.*

CHAPTER 9

HOW TO PRAISE

Once I understood the importance of praise, it dawned on me that *how* we praise is just as important as *why* we praise. If we don't properly praise those around us, it will not have the impact we desire. Our goal is to inspire people to build character in order to be successful at work and at home.

Our experience with character training at Kimray has taught us there are three important steps to issuing praise.

First, *define* the character quality.

Second, *illustrate* how it was used.

Third, *explain* the benefits of demonstrating the character quality.

Defining the Character Quality

Defining the character quality helps develop a common language and improve communication. For Character First, we identified 49 character qualities and developed work-related definitions for each one (see *Appendix A*).

No Magic Number

Frequently leaders ask, "Why 49? Why not 10 or 12 or 24?"

My response is simple. "Read the list and tell me which of the 49 character qualities you don't want your employees to learn. Forgiveness? Contentment? Gratefulness? Compassion?

Tolerance? Loyalty? Which character qualities would you like to omit?" After reviewing the list, they see the need for every single one.

In fact, there are many more character qualities and different terms that describe moral traits, but the 49 qualities we started with has worked well for Kimray and many other organizations.

Getting Through the List

Many leaders quickly recognize that if you emphasize one character quality per month, it will take about four years to cover all 49. Their concern is that it will take too long. However, we spend a month on each character quality to allow time to learn and apply it. What's most important in influencing employees is your ongoing, consistent emphasis on character. Teaching the specifics of all 49 character qualities is of secondary importance.

Others wonder, "After you work through the list, does that mean you are finished?" No. Character development is never complete. It is a life-long journey. When you have taught all forty-nine character qualities, you repeat the process.

This is important for several reasons. There may be new employees who did not hear the character quality the first time it was taught. There may be employees who forgot what they learned earlier; this is an opportunity to refresh the concept and keep the emphasis on continued learning. There may also be new applications or examples that will help the employees understand the importance of character.

I'm often asked to come to organizations and cover one or more character qualities that the management feels the employees need to learn. Although there is nothing sacred about the order of the qualities, it is important not to target specific people or problems. I strongly recommend teaching all 49 character qualities in an unbiased order. Don't teach to individual problems.

Illustration

The second step is to give an illustration of how the person demonstrated the quality. Explain the specific words, actions, or attitudes he or she exhibited that motivated the praise. These can range from heroic actions such as saving someone's life, to small deeds such as encouraging a co-worker.

These illustrations require a supervisor's ability to look for the good in employees. We should give our supervisors the tools to develop the ability to see good in employees. Over the last 18 years, many of the supervisors at Kimray have become experts at being attentive and alert to those under their care.

Benefit

Explaining the benefits is the third step in praising for character. We tell how words, actions, or attitudes have positively impacted others.

If an employee arrives on time, you can praise her for punctuality by saying, "I appreciate your punctuality. Punctuality is showing esteem for others by doing the right thing at the right time. You demonstrated respect for others by being on time."

A co-worker who is cheerful in spite of difficult circumstances can be praised by telling her, "I noticed your joyfulness today. Joyfulness is maintaining a good attitude, even when faced with unpleasant circumstances. We've had a difficult day, but you were joyful, and this helped everyone around you to have a better attitude."

If they are reliable—praise for *responsibility*.

If they follow directions—praise for *obedience*.

If they are organized—praise for *orderliness*.

Learning to recognize and praise for character isn't difficult, but it requires commitment. It is easier to be committed when you understand the remarkable impact on others.

Seeing the Impact

My wife is great at praising for character. Our grandchildren live nearby, and they visit us frequently. There is seldom just one at our house, as they usually arrive with their siblings or cousins.

When my wife sees one of them display good character, she is quick to praise it. When a child gets out the Dustbuster to sweep up after dinner, she says, "Thank you for your initiative in helping me clean up. Initiative is doing something needful without being told. I didn't have to say a thing. Now we'll be done faster."

When one of the boys opens a door for us, she says, "Wow, what a man—what a gentleman." She wants them to associate their manliness with their responsibility to be gentle.

Once, a grandchild helped her clean the sofa. After just a few swipes with the sweeper, she said, "You are doing such a thorough job. You're going up and down, up and down, and not leaving any of the material unswept. It's really going to be clean after you finish." The genuine praise not only encouraged the child, but it also motivated him to continue doing a good job.

When grandchildren arrive and begin playing with toys, she praises them for being generous. "Thank you for being generous with the toys and making sure your brothers and sisters have something to play with. That makes me happy and them happy." Praise encourages children to continue in that vein a little longer before they may be tempted to be selfish.

You might think that young children would not understand and appreciate praise when you use "grownup" words like diligence, determination, thoroughness, and cautiousness. You should see how they respond—they beam as if a light were turned on inside their little faces. They may not understand the meaning of the words at first, but they sense the approval and quickly learn the character qualities and the actions that elicit positive recognition and praise.

Employees, co-workers, and spouses respond the same way. They may not be as transparent as children, but they beam on the inside.

> *In school*—*you get what you test.*
>
> *At work*—*you get what you require.*
>
> *With people*—*you get what you praise.*

New Skills Require Practice

Praising for character may not come naturally or easily for many of us. In fact, rather than looking for the good in others, we have been taught to look for mistakes and correct them. This makes us appear to be critical and negative, rather than positive and encouraging. If we are going to become proficient at this new skill, we need to learn how to praise for character—and then practice it. I would encourage you to start developing this new skill immediately. The more frequently you praise others, the easier it will become and the greater the impact will be. Two Character Recognition Guides follow. The first is an example and the second is for your use. Please don't skip this important exercise; you can start encouraging good character today.

Sample

Character Recognition Guide

Select a family member, employee, or coworker whose character you would like to recognize and encourage. Then fill in the three steps of praise below.

Name: _Thomas E. Smith_   **Date:** _December 1, 2010_

1. **Definition:** *Select a character quality that this individual regularly demonstrates and give the definition.*
Character Quality: _Initiative vs. Idleness_

Definition: _Recognizing and doing what needs to be done before I am asked to do it._

2. **Illustration:** *Give a specific illustration of how the selected character quality is demonstrated.*
Researching and reporting on methods of tracking engineering changes.

3. **Benefit:** *How does this character quality, as exhibited in this individual's life benefit you and/or others?*
This report will provide the information that management needs to make a decision.

Take the next step: Go to the person and praise them for character.

Character Recognition Guide

Select a family member, employee, or coworker whose character you would like to recognize and encourage. Then fill in the three steps of praise below.

Name: _____ **Date:** _____

1. **Definition:** *Select a character quality that this individual regularly demonstrates and give the definition.*
Character Quality: _____

Definition: _____
_____
_____

2. **Illustration:** *Give a specific illustration of how the selected character quality is demonstrated.*

_____
_____
_____

3. **Benefit:** *How does this character quality, as exhibited in this individual's life benefit you and/or others?*

_____
_____
_____

Take the next step: Go to the person and praise them for character.

Additional Character Recognition Guides
can be downloaded at:
www.characterfirst.com/downloads

CHAPTER 10

THE GOAL

The goal of Character First is to make *individuals* successful. I know now that an individual's character determines his or her success. If we help people build good character, their decisions, attitudes, and actions will be correct, even during difficult times, and they will become more successful.

Programs that improve the bottom line of an organization benefit everyone. Unfortunately, some employees view those programs as a benefit only to the owners and managers, and as harassment to them. Programs that are designed to improve the organization are frequently seen as interfering with "getting the work done."

Alphabet Soup

Kimray tried many programs to make the company more successful, including Single-Minute Exchange of Die (SMED) to reduce set-up times and to improve productivity and profitability. We created Quality Circles to review and change procedures to improve our products and service quality. We implemented just-in-time (JIT) inventory and manufacturing to reduce inventory, and we minimized work-in-process (WIP) to improve profitability and deliveries. We also used Continuous Improvement, Six Sigma, Cell Manufacturing, and many others. I think we ran the gamut of the "alphabet soup" programs, all designed to make the company more successful.

All the programs were good, and they have a place in improving an organization. But no matter how good a program is, it takes people to make it successful. If those implementing the program have poor character, it will have limited success.

Focusing on Others

Our employees are smart. They know when we are doing something that primarily benefits the organization. They also know that programs come and go. If they don't like a program, they can keep quiet, play ball, and eventually it will be gone. Long-time employees may have outlasted many programs.

Some of those programs are designed primarily to make the organization successful. Others focus on self-improvement or on "fixing" employees. They assume that employees are broken, and if you fix them, business will improve.

Character First is designed primarily to make employees successful, which is the major difference between it and most programs, including other character initiatives. Character First is others oriented. It focuses on how we can inspire others to improve their character and be more successful. It is for everyone in the organization, from the CEO to every officer, supervisor, and employee.

> *Be just as enthusiastic about the success*
> *of others as you are about your own.*
> Christian Larson

Character Is Never Static

Everyone in an organization is continually building character. The only question is whether a person is building good character, or tearing it down and replacing it with bad character. Lou Holtz, the well-known college football coach said, "You're either growing or dying—'maintaining' doesn't count."

That is true about your character. Your character is not static. The seemingly "little" decisions you make every day are either building your character or tearing down the character you have. We need to be intentional about building good character.

> *I am what I am today because of the*
> *choices I made yesterday.* Unknown

Remember, our character is like the root system of a tree. The deeper and healthier the root system of a tree, the stronger and more fruitful the tree will be. If the tree has a weak, diseased root system, it will be unhealthy and bear little or no fruit. To produce better fruit, we feed and water the roots of the tree. We know the roots are healthy when better fruit blossoms.

Just as fruit gives an indication of the condition of the roots of a tree, our attitudes, words, and actions signal the nature of our character. Just as strengthening the roots of a tree helps it produce better fruit, strengthening the character of an individual helps produce better words, actions, and attitudes.

> *Character is like a tree and reputation like*
> *its shadow. The shadow is what we think of*
> *it; the tree is the real thing.* Thomas Paine

Appealing to Human Traits

Character First succeeds because it is built around several important human traits.

First, when you honor people for character, it encourages them to build more character. It is like a snowball. Once you start it rolling, it grows and grows.

Second, people have a natural desire to please those they respect, whether it is a teacher, parent, or supervisor. That is why we recommend that supervisors praise employees on a daily basis. They are the people closest to our employees and the ones the employees want to please. Praising for character gives a clear roadmap of what is important to the supervisor and tells the employees how they can be successful in their job.

Third, people need you to reinforce the qualities that you value. At Kimray, we emphasize one character quality a month. Our supervisors talk about it, it is described in our monthly newsletter, and electronic boards throughout the plant display the character quality and its definition. In addition, we recognize employees for different qualities at our employee meetings. In every meeting we define and explain the benefits of many character qualities, and this helps our employees understand and remember them.

Finally, employees need to know what is happening in the company. They want to know they are a part of something important and are contributing to its success. Praising for character is a great way to keep your employees in the loop and let them know they are valued.

Comparative surveys have been taken of both employees and managers to see what gives employees job-related satisfaction. Managers generally think that compensation is the primary factor in employee job satisfaction. The more someone makes, the happier he should be.

Surprisingly, compensation frequently ranks fifth or sixth for employees. The idea of feeling appreciated is almost always near the top. In fact, on a list compiled by a career specialist, "Seven Things Employees Want Most at Work," the number-one thing employees want is *appreciation*. Praise heads the list for many workers in the search for happiness. Number two is *respect*.[8] Employees want to feel they are contributing to the success of the company, and they want their efforts recognized. Yet we seldom express to our employees what they are doing correctly and why we appreciate them. Praising employees helps fulfill these desires and gives you a chance to express the importance of each and every employee.

Character Determines Success

I have given examples of how Kimray has benefited from emphasizing character. Other organizations might want to implement Character First to see positive changes and to receive financial benefits. Those benefits do not come from Character First. They come from having employees of good character.

When you help your employees be successful, they will make you successful.

Successful individuals make successful families.

Successful families make successful organizations.

Successful individuals, families, and organizations make successful cities, states, and countries.

Character determines success.

CHAPTER 11

THE BEGINNING

Some may see the influence of Character First and think, "They had it wired from the start. Once they decided to take action, it was an immediate success."

That's not quite how it happened.

My first mistake was not to tell anyone about my plans for months. I didn't set a date for when we would begin emphasizing good character. I had not made it a priority, because I didn't fully understand its importance. In addition, as long as I never told anyone, there was no accountability. Once I told someone and made the commitment to use character training, I had to accept the responsibility of making it work. If it were just an idea, I wouldn't have to face the uncertainty and discomfort of change.

Finally, four or five months after I decided to implement character training, I visited with my Human Resources manager. "Nancy, in January we are going to begin training our employees on good character." We talked about what it was and the benefits it would bring us. Setting a definite start date was an important step and forced me to take action.

Our first employee meeting was not a grand success. I had spoken to our supervisors and told them we were going to use monthly employee meetings to implement character training. In one of our managers' meetings, I stood up, recognized one of the supervisors for a character quality (I think it was loyalty), and sat down. I explained to them that this was how I wanted them to recognize employees in our monthly meetings. I did little else to prepare them.

Looking back, it was a terrible way to start. We should have given our supervisors more tools. It was obvious after our first meeting that we had not given them the training to help them succeed. Nevertheless, it was how we conducted our first meeting. I now recommend that you either bring in a Character First consultant or send your managers to Character First training. They will receive an overview of Character First, practice praising for character, and learn about monthly meetings. This will provide them with the training they need to be successful.

> *The fastest way to drive an employee insane*
> *is to give him or her new responsibilities*
> *and fail to provide the necessary instruction*
> *and training to do the job.* Ken Blanchard

As the years have passed, I have seen universal problems that organizations tend to face when they implement character training. It does not matter what your company does or where it is based. If you are dealing with people, you may face one or more of these problems. I share our experiences so that you can anticipate what will happen and plan your reaction.

Public Speaking

One of the first problems to surface was that some supervisors have trouble speaking in public. I have since learned that most people dread speaking in public. We did not take this into account when we started Character First, but we learned from that mistake. We now offer Dale Carnegie Training to our supervisors. The rewards are worth every penny of the investment. Our supervisors come back with experience in public speaking and—as an added benefit—they receive additional leadership training.

What Character?

Sometimes it takes a lot of thought to choose the right character quality when recognizing an employee. I remember one supervisor who came to me with a problem. "I am supposed to recognize an employee this month, but I can't think of any positive character qualities he has displayed."

My first thought was, "If he doesn't display any positive character qualities, why is he working here?" The supervisor and I talked about possible qualities to look for, and he agreed to re-evaluate the employee. A day or two later, the supervisor came back and described several positive qualities the employee had displayed. The employee was recognized and praised at the next meeting. I watched the employee as he came up and accepted his character certificate. I remember it like it was yesterday. He was a middle-aged man, and as he shook his supervisor's hand, a tear rolled down his cheek. Someone later told me why the employee had become so emotional. He said it was the first time the employee could remember anyone saying something positive about him.

> *Each person has his own strong points.*
> Aesop

Not Me!

We also did not realize that some people are not comfortable receiving praise. One employee had worked for us almost a year, and the time was approaching for him to be recognized. He informed his supervisor that he did not want to be publicly praised.

His supervisor responded, "You've worked here for almost a year and have attended 11 meetings. You may not understand it now, but this is a positive benefit for you. We want you and your co-workers to know how much we appreciate you. Besides, I don't have a choice. This is a part of who we are at Kimray."

Rather than being publicly recognized, the man quit. He was fairly young and I'm sure he did not have trouble finding another job, but this serves as a powerful reminder that some people will have a difficult time being publicly praised.

Today, we include an explanation of Character First and our monthly meetings in our new-employee orientation. That way, everyone who joins our team understands our commitment to character training, what that includes, and therefore what to expect. In addition, we explain the purpose of public praise. If potential employees see this as a problem, they can make a decision about employment then rather than later.

Just for the record, in 18 years of Character First at Kimray, we have never had another person refuse to be recognized.

Honor

We need to be sensitive and do everything possible to make praise a positive experience. One morning I received a phone call from an employee's wife who was upset. "Why did you make fun of my husband this morning in the employee meeting?" she asked. At first I didn't know what she was talking about. Then I remembered what happened.

The man's supervisor had called him to the front to be recognized. As the employee was walking to the front of the room, the supervisor began telling a joke. Just as the employee arrived at the front and turned around, the supervisor gave the punch line and everyone laughed. The employee thought they were laughing at him.

We now train our supervisors that meetings are not a time for levity. When you praise a person, you are honoring him or her. You want to be pleasant but serious. We don't want to create any opportunity for something to be misunderstood.

This was also another reminder that some supervisors are uncomfortable speaking before a group. The supervisor was trying to be funny to take up time and to cover his anxiety. Once supervisors become confident speaking in public, they won't feel the need to tell jokes to fill the silence. Good, clean humor may be appropriate on certain occasions—but use it with caution and discretion.

Active Resistance

Another issue we faced is that some supervisors may refuse to praise their employees. One day I received a phone call from the president of a company that had adopted Character First. "I have a problem with one of our supervisors," he lamented. "It is time for him to recognize one of his employees, but he's refusing to do it."

A question popped into my head. "Have you had any other problems with this supervisor?"

The voice at the other end of the phone sighed. "We've had dozens of problems with him. But he is important to us because he manages one of our major projects. He's the only one who understands most of it, and without him we won't be able to finish it on time. He is indispensable to us."

I paused for a moment. "Well, I think that character is important to you and your company. If you are going to change the culture of your company, everyone has to be on board. You can't allow any exceptions."

I sensed the CEO's resolve grow. "You're right. I know what I need to do," he said as he hung up.

He called me back the next week and told me what had happened. He had called the supervisor into his office. "Character training is a part of our company. You are a supervisor, and one of your responsibilities is to recognize your employees." After a brief discussion, the supervisor reluctantly agreed to recognize one of his employees at the next meeting.

When everyone returned to work the following Monday, they discovered the supervisor had cleaned out his desk, lock, stock, and barrel. He had *quit in the middle of the night* rather than give genuine praise to one of his subordinates. The president of the company later told me it was the best possible solution. It resolved all of the problems that the supervisor caused. It was difficult at first, but other character-driven employees accepted the challenge, finished the project on time, and completely satisfied the customer.

That story always reminds me that no one is indispensable, regardless of position or tenure. If anyone starts to act as if he or she is irreplaceable, you need to address it because it is a sign of poor character.

Passive Resistance

When we started character training, we faced the natural resistance that comes with any change. Transformation is always difficult. It is difficult for the employer to initiate change leading to transformation, but it's also difficult for employees to adapt to change. Some employees will shrug their shoulders and take the attitude, "Here comes another crazy program that somebody dreamed up. But it's just a program, like all the others I have seen. I was here before this program, and I will be here after it is gone. All I have to do is outlast it." And they smile, nod, and pretend to be on board, but you never really know if they are committed to character training.

A year after we implemented Character First, a supervisor asked if he could say something at the beginning of the monthly meeting. I wasn't sure what to do. He hadn't spoken to me in advance about it, and I had no idea what he was going to say. I decided to let him talk, as I knew he was free to talk to the employees as soon as the meeting was over. "At least I will know what he said," I thought.

I held my breath as he stood in front of all of the employees. "When we started Character First, I thought it was going to be just another program," he said. "But after the first year, I am so glad we did it." He spent the next few minutes talking about the difference character training had made in the company and how much more satisfying and rewarding his job had become. That was a tremendous validation for character training. Even though it had taken a year, I knew he was totally committed to Character First. I would never again have to worry about what he would say.

As with any change implemented in an organization, expect some skepticism and passive resistance. But if you are doing the right thing and it is best for the organization and the employees, just be prepared to explain, train, and move forward. Time will prove you right—or wrong. But don't let fear paralyze you.

Inconsistency

Another important lesson we learned is that often we were inadvertently reinforcing an employee's character—or lack of it—in other ways. For example, we had been failing to take character into account when promoting employees or providing other rewards.

Many of our machines cost over a million dollars. Whenever we get a new one, the machinists are excited to see who is assigned as the operator. It is considered an honor. There is a strong pecking order among machinists, and those with the highest technical skills expect to be promoted to new machines. This is true among many of the skilled trades.

Several years ago, we purchased a new Computer Numerically Controlled (CNC) machine, and one of our supervisors had to decide who would have the privilege of operating it. Before he announced his decision, I asked him which employee he had selected. The supervisor told me the employee's name, and I realized it was a fast worker with excellent skills—but also with a terrible attitude.

"I don't want to send the wrong message," I told the supervisor. "All of the other employees are watching to see who will be assigned to the new CNC. They think of this as a reward. We need to make sure we take character into account." We talked for a few more minutes, and the supervisor agreed to re-evaluate his choice.

There was another employee in the same department whose work was also excellent. He didn't appear to be as fast, but his consistency and diligence more than compensated. In addition, he consistently displayed excellent character. After considering the impact of the decision, the supervisor assigned the machine to the employee who displayed good character.

Employees need to know that character is more important than skill, regardless of how small the decision may seem. Don't send mixed messages to your employees.

Hate Mail

Whenever you initiate change, some employees will not be happy and will take the opportunity to grind their axes. And a few of them will not be open or transparent with their comments.

When we started Character First, the occasional hate mail really caught me by surprise. By writing anonymously, the authors felt free to stretch the truth and use emotional language. It was painful for me to read this letter, and other companies who implement Character First may receive similar messages.

To encourage you during these trying times, I have included one of the infamous (unedited) letters I received two years after starting Character First at Kimray. It was distributed widely throughout our manufacturing plant.

PLANT NEWSLETTER

Are you content???

The plant workers have heard a lot about contentment in the past year of 93. Management seems to think that if they keep up the barrage of contentment tactics, it will eventually sink in and we will become happy little clones. The truth of the matter is, many of us have not had a pay raise in the past eight to fifteen years.

Management has stated that inflation has gone up 3% a year for the past seven years. This means the factory workers have endured a 21% loss in income by remaining loyal to Kimray. Unfortunately, the businesses we patronize are unconcerned about our dilemma and continue to raise the prices of good and services.

Management keeps stating that our profits are higher than ever, our production is greater than ever, and we are shipping more parts than anytime in Kimray history. The workers on the floor are called "world class" by management, yet we still receive no permanent pay increase.

We are told to be content, but lets look at contentment from management's point of view. They are yet to be content with our production of parts. They continue to add more and more machines for the operators to run. Our cycle times are constantly monitored to see where we might make up a few seconds. Now, we see that management is not content to pay for our spouses health insurance, which is actually another cut in pay to the employee.

The monthly meetings have become a source of irritation for the plant workers. We are shown figures in black and white of how much profit Kimray is making each month (enough to buy a Holiday inn), yet none trickles down to the worker out on the floor in the form of a permanent pay raise.

Kimray is obviously using the downturn of the global economy as an excuse to withhold permanent pay increases to the very people who are responsible for their financial success. Never has a company had more dedicated and long term employees than Kimray. It is a shame that Kimray management mouths the words "world class," but that is as far as it goes. Bonuses may be given or taken away at any time. Management will not even discuss a permanent pay raise with its employees, which shows where their heart really is...making money.

Kimray does not mind spending money on new vehicles, new machinery, computer equipment, or as the newspaper said, "old Holiday Inns." Yes, we believe

```
the Kimray workers are world class,
unfortunately management has not seen
fit to raise our salary to that level.
How long will we let Kimray call us
"world class" workers, but treat us
like second class citizens? Let's not
remain silent any longer! For your sake,
and for the benefit of your family, let
management know how you feel.
```

Fortunately, I was alone when I read the letter—my immediate response would not have been considered "good character." But good character requires that we respond to criticism appropriately, so I spent some time thinking about how to respond.

An old proverb says, "Where there is smoke, there is fire." I knew that the vast majority of the letter was untrue and that most of our employees were not disgruntled. Even so, I considered this letter to be "smoke" and worthy of careful review to determine if there was even one percent of truth that needed to be addressed.

I made copies of the letter, called a meeting of my top managers, and explained my desire to carefully review it. It was extremely important to identify and correct any valid criticisms. We summarized the content of the "Plant Newsletter" and distributed it throughout the management at our plant for additional evaluation. We did find some problems in our timeframe and method of reviewing employees, and changes were enacted to correct them. In our next employee meeting, we covered the shortcomings of our process, outlined our new procedures, and asked the employees for forgiveness.

A Way of Life

Emphasizing character in your personal life, home, and company is a full-time commitment. Every decision you make will either build your character or diminish your character. When you accept that and commit to building your character, to modeling character, and to inspiring character in others, it will change your view of everything and everyone.

As your character grows, it becomes the compass and the attitude indicator in your life. It gives you the direction you so desperately need in the small decisions—when it is easy to do the right thing—and also in the larger, more difficult, and defining decisions of life.

Character determines success.

CHAPTER 12

CHARACTER FIRST EMPLOYEE MEETINGS

It took us time at Kimray to learn how to conduct employee meetings that teach character effectively. If you attend our meetings now, you will notice that we pay careful attention to every detail. How you structure each meeting is critical. Each meeting should be consistent so that employees know what to expect every time.

Frequency

When I began planning our character program at Kimray, I didn't know how often to hold meetings. My first thought was to meet every morning, but I couldn't justify the expense of the manufacturing shop sitting idle. I was also worried that a daily meeting would be difficult for our employees to accept. Weekly meetings also seemed excessive.

I finally committed to monthly meetings, and it was one of the aspects of Character First that worked well from the start. In fact, nearly all organizations that have adopted Character First have found that monthly meetings work well. This schedule makes it easy to systematically focus on one character quality at a time and to ensure that every employee is recognized at least once a year.

However, some companies hold employee meetings for 5-10 minutes before each shift as part of their daily business practice. These meetings could easily be adapted to include Character First.

Location

You do not have to hold your meetings in a fancy conference room or a separate building. When we started at Kimray, we didn't have a permanent meeting place. The first few years we held our meetings in our warehouse near a loading dock. We purchased 200 red folding chairs, arranged them in rows, and set up an overhead projector and video screen. Other meetings were held in the middle of our assembly room. Today, meetings are held in a nice conference room, and the employees sit in padded Kimray red and black chairs. We offer refreshments like popcorn, coffee, and tea. These refinements are a nice touch, helping employees recognize the importance of the meetings and look forward to them. However, where you hold your meetings is a minor issue; of much greater importance is what you do during the meetings.

Starting on Time

We start and end each meeting on time to demonstrate punctuality. Each employee is expected to be present before the meeting starts. We praise the employees for being on time, which reinforces the importance of punctuality. If you wait for everyone to arrive, your meetings will not start on time. Without an expectation of punctuality, some employees will trickle in later and later.

Attendance

Our meetings are mandatory. Some companies have tried to make them voluntary and offer employees a free lunch or some kind of prize if they attend. But if you have safety meetings, are they optional? I doubt it. Character training is no less important than safety training.

Optional meetings imply that character is optional. Don't just talk about character, but demonstrate—from the top down—that character is a core value of your company. All of your employees should be required to attend character training on company time. If you only meet once a month for 30-45 minutes, it is cost-effective. The benefits far outweigh the costs.

The Leader

To send the appropriate message about the value your organization places on character, it is important for a high-level leader to conduct the meetings. Supervisors recognize individual employees during the meetings, but a senior leader needs to be the "master of ceremonies." The President of Kimray leads our meetings.

Thomas Hill III, Kimray President, Leading
a Character First Employee Meeting

Format

We have developed a strict format for our meetings. Every meeting begins with the supervisors recognizing employees who have employment anniversaries that month. We then show and explain Kimray's abbreviated financial reports, including balance sheet, profit and loss statement, and a workers' compensation report. This not only conveys our openness with our employees, but it also helps them understand profit and loss. They see each month how much profit the company has made and how each department is doing. In our workers' compensation report, we don't identify any employees who were hurt on the job, but we do report the type and cost of the accidents.

As a private company, we have no obligation to make our financial reports public. When we started this, a few skeptical employees groused, "They are just making this up, they aren't showing us the real finances." Undeterred, we continued, and in time even the staunchest skeptic became a believer. We have continued this practice for almost 20 years. Nothing creates trust like showing your organization's balance sheet to your employees.

> *A man's treatment of money is the most decisive test of his character, how he makes it and how he spends it.* James Moffat

We continue with general announcements about company policies, new programs for the employees, and any other vital information. The last 10 minutes of the meeting are used to present the character quality we will be emphasizing the following month. The entire meeting, by design, takes 45 minutes. We are always careful to finish either on time or early.

First and Last

The beginning and the ending of the meeting are the most important parts. The beginning is important because people are attentive and expectant. The ending matters because employees are more likely to remember the last thing they hear.

The employee meetings are held for the primary purposes of recognizing and praising employees on their anniversaries and introducing the character quality of the month. Many other things can also be covered, but if you have to omit something or shorten a presentation, don't shorten the time devoted to character. Adjust the "filler" to control the time of the meeting. Start and stop every meeting with a discussion of character.

Remember—the main purpose of the meeting is character.

Multiple Shifts

We had to resolve many issues to have effective employee meetings. One was how to handle multiple shifts. At Kimray, we have over 500 employees working three shifts, so it isn't practical to have every employee attend one meeting.

As a result, each smaller shift has its own meeting, and larger shifts are broken into multiple meetings. By doing this, we make sure all of our employees get the same information on the same day from the same person. We don't have to worry about miscommunication or having employees on the clock outside of their normal shift.

One company we worked with had continuous production requiring three shifts, one relieving the other. Their solution was to have the oncoming shift arrive early enough once a month to attend the employee meeting. After the meeting, they would relieve the departing shift, and those employees would stay long enough to attend their meeting. If you are committed to character training, a little creativity can solve virtually any problem.

Multiple Locations

Holding meetings for companies with multiple locations was another challenge. Kimray now has 10 separate facilities. As we grew, I wondered, "How in the world do we have meetings that include our off-site employees?" The solution was simpler than I thought.

We now video one meeting at the home office and transfer it to DVD. Within 24-48 hours it can reach each location. The managers at our remote facilities use this when they hold employee meetings, and the employees feel as if they are a part of the home office meeting. Depending on the size of the facility, they may skip certain portions of the DVD in order to have time to recognize their employees and discuss other topics.

Some companies solve the problem of multiple locations by holding conference calls with the top-level managers from all locations, in advance of the monthly employee meetings. The senior executive shares the information that the managers need to emphasize at their locations; then those managers hold the meetings with their employees.

Other companies have invested in videoconferencing or webcasting technology, which allows the senior executive to conduct at least a portion of the meeting from a central location. Typically, the meetings will be structured to allow the larger locations to "sign off" so they can lead certain parts of the meeting locally, such as employee recognition and financial reporting. With the Internet, Skype, FaceTime, and other technological advances, it is possible to conduct effective employee meetings for employees in multiple locations.

Size

Multiple meetings also reduce both the number of employees who attend each meeting and the number recognized at each meeting. Our experience is that no more than 60-80 employees should attend each meeting. Do the math and you will know why.

If you have 60 employees attending each meeting, on average there will be five employees who will be recognized. We live in a world where people are used to things happening quickly. People will only listen so long before becoming bored. It takes two to five minutes to recognize an employee. If more than five employees are recognized, you risk spending the entire meeting handing out certificates. You will lose the opportunity to discuss other important issues, and the attention of the employees will wane.

All or Nothing

Once you have made the decision to implement character training, start it, take the heat, and get it over with. Think of removing a bandage. The longer you take to pull a bandage off, the worse (and longer) it hurts. Do it in one decisive motion—don't stretch it out. Rather than preventing problems, you simply prolong them if you implement character training over a period of time. Companies that have tried to phase in character training have found it less effective because it implies that the organization is not totally committed. Partial commitment is not an option when it comes to character training.

Shortly after beginning Character First, a major food distributor in Australia discovered that a long-time, well-respected employee had been stealing. Several high-level executives were called into a meeting to handle the issue. One of the executives said he felt the person's employment should be terminated but wanted some time to think the matter through. Another manager, who had only been at the company a short time, spoke up. "If we don't terminate this employee, then we need to change the name from Character First to Character Sometimes." The other executives knew he was right, and the right decision suddenly became clear.

Gifts

At Kimray, we give employees a small gift on their anniversaries in addition to their character certificates. It helps communicate their value to the company and makes the occasion memorable. These have been as simple as a lapel pin, a book, a paperweight with a magnifying glass, a calculator and pen set, or a Kimray barometer. Sometimes they are more extravagant, such as a framed copy of the Declaration of Independence or the Ten Commandments. The most popular gifts have been a Kimray pocketknife, a Leatherman all-purpose tool, a red Maglite flashlight, and two Kimray coffee mugs with coasters. Many employees say their all-time favorite gift was $60 cash, given to each employee during Kimray's 60th anniversary.

We also use the employee meetings to recognize employees who have perfect attendance or who have been accident-free. They might receive cash or a gift card to a restaurant to acknowledge their achievements.

Common Language

Character First creates a common language that permeates the company. Even though you emphasize only one character quality a month, you may recognize employees for three or four different qualities at each meeting. As these employees are recognized, the other employees hear the additional character qualities, their definitions, and how they are demonstrated.

Different people attach different meanings to words, and this can cause problems when we talk to each other. Several years ago, one of our employees had an X-ray taken of his liver. The doctor detected an abnormality and suspected it was cancer. "Where do you work?" the doctor asked. The man told him he worked at Kimray.

The doctor assumed it was "*Chem*ray" and queried, "Do you work with chemicals?"

"I only know of one," the man said and told him the name of it.

The doctor shook his head. "I don't know anything about that chemical, but it could be the cause."

The man came to work the next day and started telling people that he was dying from liver cancer caused by chemicals used in our plant. He also told them that if they worked with the chemical, they were going to get cancer and die, too. Within a few hours, the plant was in an uproar. (Further tests revealed that the first tests were in error. He did not have a spot on his liver. He did not have cancer. And he died of old age many years later.)

After learning he had upset many of our employees, I called the man into my office and commented, "I don't think that was very loyal."

"Loyal?" he questioned. "How can you say I'm not loyal when I've worked here for over 35 years?" For him, loyalty was synonymous with length of service.

The Character First definition of loyalty is, "Using difficult times to demonstrate my commitment to those I serve." That means when you see a problem or think you have been wronged, you give me the opportunity to resolve the situation before you talk to others about it.

Character training develops a common vocabulary so everyone understands when you talk about punctuality, attentiveness, or flexibility. It is your job to communicate clearly and to make sure people understand you. Using a common language of character helps accomplish this.

Application Sessions

When we started character training at Kimray, everything was new, fresh, and exciting. We continued praising for character, holding monthly meetings, and distributing Character

First materials to each employee. Many employees took the materials home and used them with their families. We saw great things happen as the culture of our company improved. But we are always looking for ways to add value and to improve the personal application and retention of our training.

One proven method of improving retention is to discuss new ideas soon after they are taught. This works well with 5-10 employees but is impractical in an employee meeting with 60 or more employees. We felt that not being able to hold discussions after each meeting was limiting the effectiveness of our character training. Larry Rhoads, Director of Character First at that time, observed the same problem in many organizations. He helped resolve this by recommending what we now call "application sessions."

Application sessions are very simple and require little or no training for the participants. Within a week after the monthly employee meeting, the supervisor holds a meeting with all of the employees who report to her. This smaller group takes the Character First materials and spends 15-20 minutes discussing the character quality using the discussion questions. This enables each individual to participate in a meaningful dialogue about the character quality of the month.

In addition, participants are challenged to recall a recent example from the workplace when someone demonstrated the character quality and explain the benefits to the individual, the employees, or the company. As an alternative, they may recollect an incident when the character quality was violated and the negative results that followed. This dialogue and the workplace examples help make the character quality personal and memorable. The supervisor usually leads the discussion, but in some instances, the group allows each member to have a turn leading the conversation.

At Kimray, we have found the application sessions to be a valuable extension of the employee meetings, and we have continued them for about 6 years. Many other organizations have also found them to be an important component of their Character First programs.

Benefits of Character First Meetings

Employee meetings offer many benefits:

- They provide an organized method to recognize employees publicly.
- They give time to introduce the new character quality for the upcoming month.
- They serve as a review of the character qualities.
- They allow you the opportunity to present anniversary gifts.
- Employees have the chance to get to know employees from other departments, and new employees have the opportunity to meet long-time employees.
- They demonstrate the opportunity for promotion in the organization.
- They provide a time to present a financial summary of the organization.
- They are an opportunity to explain profit, loss, expenses, and other business concepts.
- They provide an opportunity to talk about important issues such as safety and health insurance and to make announcements about the organization.
- They give managers training and experience in speaking to a larger audience.

In summary, Character First employee meetings provide the opportunity to honor employees, provide character training, and disseminate important information about the organization. Conducted right, the meetings are a win-win situation for everyone.

CHAPTER 13

PUBLIC RECOGNITION

Public recognition is a way to praise, honor, and demonstrate respect for an employee. Over a period of months, we developed the following guidelines that anyone can use to publically recognize and honor an individual.

Preparation

The more you know about an individual, the easier it is to praise him or her. Don't wait until the week before the recognition. Do your preparation throughout the year. Invest the time and truly honor the individual.

Get to know the employee and ask questions about her family. Research the meaning of her name. Learn about her hobbies, likes, and dislikes. What is her background with the organization, how long has she worked here, what are her jobs, and what promotions has she earned? What is her educational background? Does she have any technical training? What organizations does she belong to? Does she do volunteer work?

Think of word pictures to illustrate unique work situations in a way that communicates a principle that is easily understood and applied by all. For example, "Susie's job is coordinating the flow of work orders to the machine shop. She determines what job goes on what machine and when. She is like a traffic cop, providing the direction that keeps the work flowing smoothly.

She has a bird's eye view of the overall schedule. If we don't follow her direction, it will likely cause our schedule to crash."

Write out what you plan to say. As author and speaker Elisabeth Elliot said, "You never really know what you are thinking until you write it down." I believe that applies here.

The following is an example of completing a Character Recognition Worksheet to prepare for a public recognition. The information on the Character Recognition Worksheet can be used later to prepare a Character Certificate.

Example Character Recognition Worksheet

The goal of character recognition is to encourage each individual to reach his or her full potential by praising positive character. With thoughtful and thorough preparation, you can ensure this is a memorable and positive experience. The appreciation and encouragement individuals feel for having their character praised more than compensates for the extra time and energy expended to make this a special event.

Name: *Use the individual's given name rather than a nickname.*
Thomas E. Smith

Anniversary Date:
December 1, 1996

Years of Service:
14 years

Introduction: *Include appropriate information about family, hobbies, special interests, and meaning of name.*
Thomas has a wife and two children. They are
expecting their third child, a son. He enjoys golfing,
fishing, and camping with his family. He spends a lot of
time with his children and coaches some of their sports.

Responsibilities: *Give a brief history of the time with the organization, current position, and responsibilities.*

Thomas started part-time while in high school. After graduation, he worked in the machine shop while taking drafting courses at night. He transferred to the drafting department where he has worked for the last six years and was recently promoted to senior draftsman.

1. Definition: *Select a character quality that this individual regularly demonstrates and give the definition.*

Character Quality: Initiative vs. Idleness

Definition: Recognizing and doing what needs to be done before I am asked to do it.

2. Illustration: *Give a **specific** illustration of how the selected character quality is demonstrated.*

Thomas demonstrates initiative in many ways, on the job as well as in his personal life. As an example, he recently saw the need for a better method to track our engineering changes. On his own, he researched various methods and then prepared a report summarizing the strong and weak points of each system. After reviewing his report, we were able to select and then implement the system that best suited our needs.

3. Benefit: *How does this character quality, as exhibited in this individual's life, benefit you and/or others?*

This new system has improved the accuracy of our engineering records. We are able to quickly determine what changes have been made to each product and why. This keeps us from returning to old processes that we have abandoned because they didn't work and helps us keep our engineering drawings up-to-date. This saves money and improves the quality of our product.

Conclusion: *Thank you, Thomas, for your initiative and your 14 years of service.*

Scott D. Thatcher	*December 1, 2010*
Supervisor	Date

Character Certificate

When we began to recognize each Kimray employee annually, we wanted to make it special. We also wanted to give the employee a reminder of the recognition. Our solution was to create an individualized character certificate to give to the employee, and we put a copy in the employee's personnel record.

The character certificate is very simple. It is similar to any certificate you might receive at a graduation or at the completion of a course of instruction. In the beginning, we purchased plain blank certificates from the store. Now, Character First offers beautiful blank character certificates that any organization can use.

The front of the certificate has the person's name, the character quality, and the definition of the character quality. For example:

XYZ, Inc. recognizes

Thomas E. Smith

for the Character Quality of

Initiative

Recognizing and doing what needs to be done before I am asked to do it.

Scott D. Thatcher	December 1, 2010
Supervisor	Date

At Kimray, we even take the extra step of affixing a gold seal to the front and embossing it with the corporate seal.

On the reverse side of the certificate, we print the character recognition written by the supervisor. It is important to give careful consideration to what is written. This becomes a future character reference for the employee.

To continue the example:

"Thomas has now worked here at XYZ, Inc. for 14 years. He started as a part-time employee in the machine shop, went to night school to learn the job of a draftsman, was promoted to the drafting department, and was recently promoted to Senior Draftsman.

Thomas is being recognized today for Initiative: Recognizing and doing what needs to be done before I am asked to do it.

Thomas recently saw the need for a better method to track engineering changes. He researched different solutions and prepared a report for management. The report enabled management to select the best system for our company. The new system has given us an ability to track changes accurately and keep our drawings up-to-date. This saves money and improves the quality of our product.

Thank you, Thomas, for 14 years of service, for your friendship, and for your initiative."

Character Certificate Benefits

There are five major benefits from giving a character certificate to an employee.

- **The certificate conveys in written form what was publicly stated.** Frequently, the employee is excited and may remember the feeling of the moment, but not all that was said. The character certificate is a detailed, personal reminder of when and why the employee was recognized.

- **The certificate communicates to the employee's family the value of the employee to the company.** On several occasions, weeks and even months after an employee was recognized, his or her spouse would meet me and could quote almost verbatim what was written on the certificate. Honoring employees with public recognition and character certificates can have a tremendous impact on their family.

- **The character certificate is a source of continuing encouragement to the employee.** As I visit companies that use Character First and that publically recognize employees with character certificates, I frequently see employees displaying the certificates in their workspaces. They are proud of their certificates because they are tokens of appreciation, reminders of the good character they demonstrate, and encouragement to continue building good character.

- **A copy of the character certificate creates a permanent record in the employee's personnel file.** What do you usually find in an employee's personnel file? The employment application, records of pay raises and vacation time, and records of what the employee has done wrong. Seldom is there anything positive. The character certificate is a positive addition to the file. After a few years, this can become significant.

- **The character certificate builds a portfolio of character references for the employee.** It is difficult to get references from former managers and employers. After working for a few years at a Character First company, employees have several character references from their immediate supervisor. If they change jobs, they have several character references to take to an interview. This may be the most important benefit of character certificates to some employees.

> *Your best résumé is not what you write, but how you live.* Unknown

Introduction

An individual's name is very important. Introduce the employee using their given name, not just a nickname, and be sure to pronounce the name correctly. In some companies, employees seldom find an occasion to become acquainted with individuals who work in other departments. The anniversary of an employee is an opportunity to introduce the employee to everyone attending the meeting.

You can give information about the employee's family, relate hobbies and special interests, give some history of the employee's time with the company, and explain their responsibilities. It is important to share only information that is suitable for public knowledge. If you are uncertain whether or not you should share certain information, ask the employee. If there is any doubt, do not give the information.

> *I have never been hurt by something*
> *I didn't say.* Calvin Coolidge

Recognition

The recognition is the information written on the character certificate. Reading the recognition is perfectly acceptable if it helps supervisors stay "on track."

Definition: Begin the recognition by reading the character quality and its definition.

Illustration: Give one or more examples of how the employee demonstrated the character quality. You could relate the specific challenges of the employee's current job responsibilities with the character qualities necessary to perform that job successfully. You may want to mention additional character qualities, but give special attention to the character quality highlighted by the character certificate. Remember, this character quality does *not* need to be the same quality on which the organization is focusing for the month.

Benefit: Benefits may include how the employee's character impacted you, other employees, customers, the company, or the community.

Summary

Don't compare one person's character with others. Avoid using terms of comparison such as "the best," "the most," or "more than."

Maintain an attitude of sincerity. Avoid levity, joking, and jesting. The goals of public praise are to show genuine appreciation for this person—to communicate honor, to explain her value to the company, and to use her character as a positive example.

And finally, be concise. If you prepare properly, two or three minutes will generally suffice to recognize an individual. If there are five or six people to be recognized, this will take 15-20 minutes. This is about as long as you want to spend on the recognition portion of the meeting. Even so, special circumstances may warrant spending more time on an individual recognition.

CHAPTER 14

TEACHING AND MODELING CHARACTER

At Kimray, we knew we couldn't force people to change. We had tried that and failed, and we had a book full of rules to prove it. We had to learn to inspire people so that they would want to build good character. The first step was defining character. Then we needed to understand how to model, teach, and inspire character.

We started by explaining to our employees that good character determines all long-term success. When we look at history and study those who have made a positive, enduring impact on our society, there is a common thread that runs through their lives. They were people of good character. They were not perfect by any measurement, but they learned from their mistakes and listened to their inner compasses to get on the right track.

We had to demonstrate that our success is determined in large part by our individual character. Our interest in developing character has always been to help others be successful. There may be other benefits, but our primary desire was—and still is—to help our employees and their families succeed.

Why was this so important? Most people never think about character or what it means in their lives. Few companies ever address character issues with their employees. Recognizing the importance of character and understanding how to teach and model character are the reasons why Character First has made such an impact around the world. People are motivated by seeing good character modeled, but they need effective teaching to understand it and transfer it into their attitudes, words, and actions.

Reaping Positive Character Qualities

I had the privilege of growing up across the street from my grandmother. She had a garden and often needed help. She would call me over, and it was my responsibility to plow the furrows, plant the seeds, hoe for weeds, and gather the produce. From her simple garden, I learned some of life's most valuable lessons.

Together we would stretch a string from one end of the garden to the other. Using a push-plow, I would make a furrow along that line. As I planted the seeds, she would tell me the importance of putting the seeds in the bottom of the furrow. If I planted them all on the bottom, the plants would

Tom with Grandmother

grow in one straight line. If I put them to one side or the other, the plants would grow in a zigzag pattern.

When weeds grew with the plants, she would call me and have me hoe or pull them out. Then she would stand with me at the end of the row. "Look down there. Look how pretty that is," she would say. "There are no weeds, just the pretty plants in a straight line."

One year, my grandmother and I got a peck (1/4 of a bushel) of seed potatoes. We cut them into pieces, making sure there was an "eye" in each one. I planted them but didn't always make sure they were straight. When that happened, my grandmother would gently pull me aside and show me how the row was crooked. As the plants grew, my job was to pick off the potato bugs and worms before they caused any damage.

Our peck of seeds yielded four bushels of potatoes during a single harvest. This was sixteen times the quantity of potatoes we planted. One of the potatoes was *huge*. It was so big that my grandmother called the local newspaper. A reporter came out, took a picture of the potato and the four bushels

Boy Brings in Good Potato Crop

Tommy Hill, 9-year-old son of Mrs. Lois Jean Davis, is having exceptional success with a backyard garden this season.

He decided to help out his grandparents, Mr. and Mrs. A. J. Jackson, 113 North Rowe, with their garden this year because his grandfather's health would not permit such strenuous activity. Yesterday he harvested a potato crop of four bushels, grown from a peck of seed potatoes. Some of them are very large for homegrown potatoes, bigger than a croquet ball.

Soon he'll be harvesting some cucumbers and squash.

The Pryor Jeffersonian
June 18, 1952

we had harvested, and printed the picture with an article in the local newspaper.

Working with my grandmother taught me great lessons about being diligent, reaping what you sow (potatoes grew potatoes), reaping later than you sow, and reaping more than you sow. My grandmother modeled these lessons with her actions, but I was able to remember and apply them in my life because she took time to explain them and praised my diligence when I did them correctly. She demonstrated that there were consequences for doing right and consequences for doing wrong. The consequences for doing right are always better. I was blessed to have such a powerful character model in my life. Without my grandmother teaching and modeling good character, I know that my life could have taken a different turn. Her actions and words gave me a foundation based on good character.

> *Example isn't another way to teach, it is the only way to teach.* Albert Einstein

Sharing Examples with Others

Character First emphasizes modeling character because people need to see examples. My grandmother's example was so effective, because I not only heard her teach character lessons, but I also watched her live them. Hearing a person talk about the importance of boldness or decisiveness is one thing. Watching them display boldness or decisiveness while they are under pressure is another.

My grandmother was left alone with three small children to raise, after my grandfather died during the flu epidemic of 1919. There weren't any government programs to aid her. She supported her family by doing other people's laundry and ironing, helping women care for babies, and renting out rooms in

My father is the smallest child in the wagon next to grandmother.

her home. She experienced pressure and persevered. She was a worthy example of good character.

During our monthly meetings, we introduce the character quality we will emphasize the following month. We also take the time to discuss how the character quality has impacted our personal lives and improved the environment at Kimray.

We make a point to talk about both success and failure when it comes to character. It is important to mention both on a regular basis. None of us is perfect. We all have character issues we need to resolve. If you only tell about your successes, it may drive a wedge between you and your employees. If you acknowledge your shortcomings, your employees will be more receptive to changing their character.

We teach the following guideline at Character First. When sharing a personal illustration, talk about your failures. When using an illustration about someone else, tell about her success.

> *Sharing your successes builds walls.*
> *Sharing your failures builds bridges.*

SUCCESS OF CHARACTER FIRST IN OTHER ORGANIZATIONS

We have had the privilege of introducing Character First to a variety of organizations around the world. Regardless of your type of organization, you can improve the lives of your employees and the atmosphere of your company by teaching and modeling character. Here are a few of the organizations that have used Character First and the tremendous results they have achieved.

Hollytex Carpet Mill

Workers' compensation costs are a significant part of any company's operating expenses. This is especially true for manufacturing facilities. When someone is injured on the job, it costs the company more than money. The value of the time lost to an on-the-job injury can quickly exceed the premiums of workers' compensation insurance.

HollyTex Carpet Mill in western Oklahoma was facing the challenge of skyrocketing workers' compensation costs. During the fiscal year 1992-93, one 240-employee plant spent $486,000 on workers' compensation. In addition, employees lost over 400 days due to work-related injuries.

Insurance costs were so high that the mill (and its insurance company) fought every claim that was filed, even the legitimate ones. The company was desperate to find a way to reduce costs. Focusing on profit and loss seemed to be the only solution.

In 1994, HollyTex implemented Character First. This forced the company to reevaluate what it deemed important. Management knew they had lost sight of the big picture. They changed their focus to employees, not just the bottom line. The employees felt more valued and began to think about how their behavior impacted the rest of the company. They also began to demonstrate character qualities such as alertness and attentiveness, which had very dramatic and tangible results. The mill's workers' compensation costs dropped to $47,000 during fiscal year 1994-95. In 1995, the number of lost-time days dwindled to five. There was a quick reduction of the company's insurance expenses.

Character First is not just another program. It is a way of life that will fundamentally change the way you and your employees look at the world, just like it did for this carpet mill and its employees.

EDG, Inc.

EDG, Inc. is an engineering consulting company with offices across the United States, as well as in Africa, Asia, and South America. The company employs over 500 engineers, designers, and project management personnel who design major construction projects, including offshore oil and gas platforms and machines that help load and unload ships in port.

Dwight Paulsen and Paul Mogabgab founded the company in 1982, because they were dissatisfied with the "bottom line" culture of the oil and gas industry. Their vision was to create a company that was based on character and was a great place for engineers to work. As the company expanded, they needed a structured methodology to maintain and transfer their culture.

One of EDG's clients recommended Character First. Company representatives attended our training seminar and recognized the value of Character First. As EDG's management became familiar with what we taught, they saw how these principles and methods could help them fulfill their vision. It would also give their employees the tools to positively impact their homes and communities.

EDG had been holding monthly employee meetings for some time, and it immediately incorporated character training. It then created and distributed monthly bulletins and sent additional employees to be trained. Character committees were eventually established, and character notebooks were distributed throughout the company.

The results have enhanced the work experience for all EDG employees, and character training has been instrumental in creating a character-based environment. The emphasis on character has dramatically decreased turnover, absenteeism, and tardiness.

EDG knows that when an organization emphasizes character, it addresses the root of employment issues. Supervisors have traditionally focused on the negative, but recognizing and praising for character creates positive relationships with employees.

Emphasizing character has also given the company a powerful recruiting tool—and a competitive advantage. EDG employees often tell others about their enhanced employment experiences, and clients and consultants have noticed the difference in dealing with EDG as opposed to other firms in the industry. Some clients have even visited EDG and attended employee meetings. Implementing character training has created opportunities for EDG it would not have known otherwise.

EDG is an example of how Character First is not a rigid "program," but rather a set of universal principles that work anywhere. EDG took the principles we identified and applied them in the most effective way for its organization. EDG's culture of character has become a recognized attribute of the company and has distinguished it from its competitors.

Ferreira Optical

A family-owned optical company in Trinidad was experiencing major ongoing problems negotiating salary and benefits with its union. The negotiations were frequently intense and combative, and the process often lasted two years. As soon as one agreement was reached, it would be time to start on the next one. This had been going on for over 18 years, and CEO Colin Ferreira was intent on finding a better way.

After coming to Oklahoma and attending a Character First training conference, his company began using Character First. The first year after implementing Character First, Ferreira Optical was able to reach an agreement with the union in three months. Management and employees alike benefited from the improved relationships. The CEO attributed the improved working relationship almost entirely to their implementation of Character First. He said his management team received the greatest impact and the greatest benefit.

Character First, when implemented properly, for the right reasons, and with the complete support and participation of management, can make a positive difference in any organization.

McDonald's Restaurant

Managing a franchised restaurant is a very challenging job. The pay for entry-level employees can be comparatively low, and typically there is a high turnover rate. This causes a continuous cycle of employee recruitment, hiring, and training. Many of the new employees have no previous restaurant or customer-service experience. In addition, some have had little opportunity to develop character qualities such as punctuality, responsibility, reliability, hospitality, and flexibility. This can lead to poor customer experience.

Reginald Jones owned three McDonald's restaurants in a major metropolitan area. The franchisor had a policy of regularly sending an evaluator to grade his restaurants based on several factors. These included the cleanliness of the restaurant, correctness of the orders, the time from when a customer walked up until he was greeted and the order taken, and the time from when the order was taken until the customer received his food. The evaluator also reviewed the franchisee's inventory storage and management, the freshness of the food, the temperature of the food, and how well trained the employees were. The grading system was "A" through "F." "A" was outstanding, and "F" was totally unsatisfactory.

On one occasion, the evaluator graded one of Mr. Jones' restaurants an "F." Mr. Jones was devastated. He asked for the location of an "A" grade restaurant to visit and see how to improve his facility. He was told there were no "A" grade restaurants in the city. Undeterred, and willing to travel if necessary, he asked for the location of an "A" restaurant anywhere in the state. Somewhat sheepishly, the evaluator said no restaurant had received a grade that high.

Mr. Jones had heard of other businesses that improved by implementing Character First, and he was convinced that character training would improve his restaurant. He knew he was facing many obstacles but courageously began teaching character to his employees twice a week.

As the time for the next restaurant evaluation approached, Mr. Jones knew the restaurant had improved tremendously. The employees were delivering better customer service, service was quicker, sales had increased 97 percent, and turnover had decreased by 200 percent compared to the previous year. Customers noticed the improvement in the store's atmosphere and frequently asked, "What has changed here?"

One store manager noted that since the character program started, "People seem to care a little bit more about the store and the customer." The attitude of the crew had changed, he said. "They're not as defensive as they used to be. They've learned to listen a little bit to what the customer is saying, and they smile while they work."

The day for the evaluation arrived. Mr. Jones was excited to see the impact of character training on the restaurant's score. Everything was measured, checked, timed, and tested as required by corporate headquarters. When the final grade was presented, Mr. Jones was excited to learn it was an "A." It was the only restaurant in the state to receive one. What was the difference between this evaluation and the previous one?

Mr. Jones had invested in his employees' success by encouraging them to develop good character. One manager stated, "On the employee side, it created a sense of unity." He added that the store operates more smoothly since it began to focus on character.

Another manager agreed, explaining that good character is a rallying point—something all employees can share regardless of their background.

An employee said Character First helped her and her co-workers to "have good attitudes" and encouraged them to "do the right things" when they come to work. Another said the Character First curriculum taught him to do more than is expected. He now aspires to learn skills and to be an asset to the store.

The employees also took home what they learned about character. One employee said she was learning to be more decisive in her everyday life, while another shared that he was able to encourage a family member to use discretion.

As the employees changed, as they became men and women of character, their interactions with the customers improved, they were better able to do their jobs, and the restaurant became successful.

> *"We tried different things through motivation, prizes, and different incentives. And those, from what I've seen, do not work. But I believe character works, because now they know we do what's right because it's right to do what's right!"*

Reginald Jones
Restaurant Owner

Regional Hospital

Hospitals are difficult places to work. The pressure of caring for critically ill patients, the long hours, and the demands of constantly performing at your best can be grueling. The staff is continuously being trained in patient care, service, procedures, and stress management. Hospitals often use quarterly patient-satisfaction surveys to rate their service and quality of care. These surveys are a key measure of the organization's success.

For one regional hospital in the greater Oklahoma City area, patient satisfaction typically scored around 75 percent. Seeking to improve patient care and help the nurses and staff develop better character at work and at home, the hospital administration made Character First an integral part of training.

After the first quarter of implementing Character First, the hospital's patient satisfaction jumped to 94 percent. After the second quarter, it rose again—to 96 percent. It stayed in that range as long as the hospital taught Character First.

However, when the renewal date approached for the hospital's accreditation, the administration focused all their resources on that task and stopped teaching Character First. Patient satisfaction dropped almost twenty percentage points the next quarter, returning to the levels where it had been prior to the hospital using character training. The hospital had been using Character First long enough to see a change in the way their nurses and staff responded, but it was not enough time to change their permanent character.

The administration resumed character training, and at the end of the next quarter, patient satisfaction again rose to over 95 percent. The CEO of the hospital stated that the high level of patient satisfaction was due to the implementation of Character First with the nurses and hospital staff.

Good Samaritan Nursing Home

When we can no longer care for a loved one, we frequently trust them to the safekeeping of a nursing home.

Nursing homes are special places—and the vast majority of them work diligently to provide exceptional care, sometimes under difficult circumstances. They often face financial pressure, because they are not always paid "fair market value" for the services they provide. It can be emotionally draining for the staff to help residents who are unable to meet their most basic needs without assistance. Dealing with family members, who may be struggling with the decision to place a relative in an extended care facility, also takes a toll.

One nursing home desired to give back to its staff and workers. The management team wanted to help the staff be successful, not just at work, but personally as well. While researching possible solutions, they discovered Character First. After learning how Character First works, they determined that by encouraging employees to build good character in their lives, they could help the employees achieve true success.

Character First came to the facilities and provided on-site training for the managers to look for and praise good character daily. In addition, we explained the importance of praising employees for character on their employment anniversaries.

One of the supervisors spoke up. "We can't do that," she said.

The trainer was accustomed to working through obstacles and asked the obvious question. "Why not?"

"Because our nursing aides don't have anniversaries," the supervisor responded. "Our turnover rate is about 100 percent, so most of our employees haven't worked here for a year." The trainer later learned that the average turnover rate for nursing aides in that state was 104 percent per year.

The trainer was stunned. "This is a nursing home, a place entrusted to care for our loved ones," he thought. "A high turnover rate means there is a constant parade of new faces for the residents to get to know. Plus, new employees are constantly trying to learn the special needs of the residents. The cost of recruiting and training new employees has to be enormous."

The trainer had a very creative idea. "Then why not recognize those that have birthdays each month?" he said. "Everyone has a birthday, no matter how long he has worked here." The managers agreed with the approach, and they began to fully implement the new character focus in the nursing home.

Many things occurred during the next 18 months, but the most amazing was that the turnover rate for nurse aides plummeted to about 6 percent. With lower turnover, recruiting and training costs tumbled, making it possible to pay higher wages. With lower turnover, the residents were able to trust and rely on the staff, and the staff learned the special needs of the residents. Lower turnover also produced a safer and more stable environment, and resident satisfaction increased.

"The staff are happy and dedicated professionals," commented the Human Resource Director. "A recent family survey we conducted showed that the families of the residents we serve overwhelmingly view us as a friendly and caring group. There is not a price tag we can put on the goodwill that we believe the Character First program has generated for our nursing center in the community."

"Character First," he continued, "has been the lynchpin in turning this nursing center into a high-quality organization."

Oklahoma County Jail

Oklahoma County has two jails. One is a juvenile facility. The other is the "regular jail" that houses all the adults. Most of the juveniles in custody are arrested for non-violent offenses, such as theft or possession of drugs. Some, however, are in for serious violent offenses, including armed robbery, rape, and murder. The juvenile facility does not have a separate area for these serious offenders; for years they were allowed to mingle with the rest of the population, putting the non-violent juveniles at risk.

A decision was eventually made to transfer the violent juvenile offenders, who were 13-17 years old, to the adult county jail. They were given a separate pod and not allowed to mingle with the adults. This meant that the juveniles were essentially on "lock-down" twenty-four hours a day. They had virtually no outside contact and no positive stimulation.

Restless Juveniles

These conditions would have been a problem for even the healthiest children, but imagine what they did to adolescents who had backgrounds that led them to rob, rape, and kill. It didn't take long for these offenders to find creative ways to alleviate their boredom.

They soon discovered that if they climbed on the tables in the common area of the pod, they could reach the ceiling. They would pull down the ceiling tiles and the metal grid that held them in place. Along with the tiles, they would bring down the sprinkler system and smoke detectors. The jailors would move them all to a different pod, but when the juveniles returned a few months later, it would start all over again.

When the sprinklers were pulled down, the broken pipes flooded the pod and damaged the ceiling tiles. Repairs, including rewiring the detectors, were expensive. A major at the jail expressed his frustration to the jail chaplain. "What are we supposed to do with these kids?" he asked.

"Why don't we teach them character?" the chaplain responded. To this day, he is not sure where he got the idea.

The chaplain bought a few books and started reading as much about character as he could. He knew the answer was out there somewhere, but he wasn't sure how to bring character into the county jail. His wife sensed his frustration and searched the word *character* on the Internet. Many of the searches referred her to Character First in Oklahoma City, where our offices at the time were only two blocks from the jail. The chaplain immediately called and scheduled a meeting with us.

Character First's new director had arrived from Indiana with his family two weeks prior to the chaplain's call. He had driven around the county jail several times and had been seriously considering how he might serve the inmates behind the walls with character training. Needless to say, he welcomed the call from the jail chaplain.

Not long afterward, Character First started a training program for the juveniles in the jail, and the chaplain observed for two weeks. He has been teaching the program in the jail ever since. The juveniles have not committed any property damage at the jail since character training began.[9]

That caught the attention of the sheriff. Although he initially thought character training was just another program that would fade away, he came to understand that character training fundamentally changes the way people think and act.

Inspiring Character in Jailors

The progress with the juvenile offenders was only the beginning of character training at the jail. A pivotal event happened one day as the chaplain watched them being locked into their cells. One of the juveniles looked at the officer closing the door and asked the chaplain, "When are you going to teach the employees around here about character?"

That question was a real blow to the chaplain. He knew and cared about the men and women who worked in the jail, and it bothered him that they were viewed as lacking character. It also bothered him because he knew that most of the juveniles had poor role models and desperately needed to learn character.

He had an idea. Central Control on the first floor operates the elevators. All the prisoners, attorneys, employees, and medical personnel have to stand and wait for the elevators to be sent. This can take a long time. The chaplain got permission to hang a poster describing character beside the door of the elevator on every floor. There's nothing else to look at, so everyone reads the posters. A Character Bulletin Board was eventually added at the employee entrance. After that, one was put in the visitors' center. Seven Character Bulletin Boards now hang throughout the Sheriff's Department.

This instilled a desire in the employees, and the idea of character spread throughout the jail. There are now two character councils, where employees are recognized in public settings, and every year there is a banquet where an employee from each of the five departments is publicly recognized for character.

What About Hardened Criminals?

Another amazing thing happened with the inmates. The jailors began housing all of the adult leaders of different gangs in the same pod. The chaplain decided he would try to teach character to these 10-12 hardened criminals.

The sheriff was concerned about the chaplain's safety and required him to be escorted into the pod by 10 guards. There were almost as many deputies as there were inmates. To everyone's surprise, the gang leaders were extremely receptive to character training. Within a month, the chaplain was able to teach with only one guard escorting him.

After a few weeks, one of the gang leaders hugged and thanked the chaplain for the training. The emphasis on character had changed his life so much that he was mailing all the materials he received to his family. He didn't want his son to follow in his footsteps.

The Results Just Snuck in the Door

What happened at the Oklahoma County Jail is a perfect example of how character training can impact any organization. The county jail operates 24 hours a day, seven days a week and deals with some of the most violent people in the world. If character training works there, it can work anywhere.

It is interesting that the chaplain had no aspirations to spread character training throughout the entire sheriff's department. Once he started it, everyone else recognized the value. "The results just snuck in the door," he explained.

The influence of Character First at the jail and in the sheriff's department was revealed to me while I was on a field trip to a science museum with my grandchildren. A museum worker brought out an eight-foot albino python for us to see and touch, and I took pictures of the children standing next to it. A man stood close by with his daughter, and I offered to photograph them with the snake. Afterward, I asked for his address so I could e-mail him the picture. When he handed his business card to me, I noticed he was an Oklahoma County deputy sheriff. I couldn't resist asking him, "I understand they have a program called Character First at the Oklahoma County Jail and in the sheriff's department. What do you think about it?"

A broad smile spread across his face. "It is the best thing we have ever done," he answered. "Not only has it helped the jail and the sheriff's department, but it has been great to take the materials home to share with my family."

It is always a delight to experience firsthand the positive impact that Character First has on organizations, families, and individuals.

Mabel Bassett Correctional Center

Oklahoma incarcerates women at nearly twice the national average. This has a huge impact on families, as well as other tax-paying citizens. If Oklahoma reduced the number of female inmates to the national average, it would save the state over $18 million per year.

Almost two-thirds of the women who are sentenced to prison have at least one child under the age of 18. This means that thousands of children are separated from their mothers. The luckier ones are taken care of by loving family members. Others are uprooted from their homes and placed into foster care and onto welfare rolls.

The Mabel Bassett Correctional Center outside Oklahoma City houses over 1,000 of the most violent female criminals in Oklahoma. They have been convicted of serious offenses, such as manslaughter, murder, armed robbery, or drug dealing.

Most are hurt, angry, and resentful. Virtually all of them come from backgrounds that view violence, abuse, and deception as the norm. Few of them grew up with positive role models. It is not uncommon for them to have suffered extreme abuse at the hands of those closest to them.

Many of these women are repeat offenders and face long, mandatory sentences. They have little incentive to behave well, because they are not eligible for any type of credit for "good behavior." They frequently assault each other and refuse to comply with the orders of the guards.

The prison's administration—noticing alarming trends, such as studies showing younger and younger girls were being incarcerated—decided that something needed to change. They wanted to help the women break the cycle of recidivism and to create a safer prison environment. The staff researched character training and discovered Character First. Because these women came from such dysfunctional backgrounds, Character First and the prison administration decided an intense and extensive program had to be developed.

Volunteering to Learn Character

In the new program at Mabel Basset, no one was required to attend character training. In fact, every interested woman had to apply to participate. She was then interviewed thoroughly to see if she was serious about changing her life.

As we were developing the prison curriculum, we received a job application from a man who had just been released from prison. He had an English degree, and we immediately saw the potential for him to help us create a curriculum for inmates. He knew the issues of prison life, the slang the inmates used, and the prison customs. He couldn't have come to us at a more valuable time, and we were very thankful to have him help us.

Two hundred women were eventually accepted into the first class. Because the culture of negative character is heavily engrained in the prison system, these women were separated from the rest of the prison population. The prison officials were concerned that if they were allowed to mingle with prisoners who were not receiving character training, they would have little chance of improving their lives. Some of the women chose to emphasize spirituality with character, and they were placed in the faith-and-character pod—nicknamed the "God pod"—while the others were placed in the character-only pod.

The women attended classes 30 hours a week for 15 months. This type of in-depth training was the only way to change the mindset of the women—to give them the freedom to choose new attitudes, thoughts, and actions.

Dramatic Results

The impact of the training at Mabel Basset has been dramatic. One year after the training started, the prison officials were extremely pleased with the results. The number of assaults has declined, and there are fewer negative interactions between the women and the guards.

The number of misconducts dropped significantly. In the year prior to participating, the women in the program had committed 169 offenses. During the time of the program, these same women committed only 69 offenses. This reflected a drop of nearly 60 percent.

The most serious offenses dropped at an even more amazing rate. In the year prior to participating in the program, the women committed 44 "class X" offenses. These involve behaviors such as possessing contraband, fighting with the guards, and injuring other inmates. Prisoners who commit these offenses can lose any earned credits and be segregated from the rest of the population for 30 days. During the program, these same women committed only eight of these offenses. This was a reduction of over 80 percent.

The results continued as women completed the training and returned to the general population of the prison. Even a year or more after completing the program, graduates continue to demonstrate the effects of character training. They have reduced the number of all misconducts by over 25 percent and "class X" offenses by over 50 percent.

The women have learned new ways to deal with their issues, and there is a waiting list to join the program. It has given the inmates purpose and direction. Most importantly, it has given them hope.

One inmate was serving time for drug distribution and possession of a firearm and had been incarcerated six times. "In all these years, this is the first time I've dealt with rehabilitation; before this, it (prison) was just housing," she said. "I always blamed others for my problems. I'm 50 years old. I've got to get home to my grandchildren." [10]

Another inmate summed up the thoughts of many. "Without this program, I wouldn't have made it," she said. "Nothing [before Character First] was changing my life." [11]

Oklahoma City Public Schools

When I grew up, schools were considered a safe place. I didn't have to worry about many of the problems our children encounter today. It never occurred to my parents that I might not come home when they sent me to school in the morning.

Things have changed, and many people are no longer able to view school as a safe haven. At many schools, children must pass through metal detectors before they can enter school. Once they get inside, there is no guarantee that the detectors have made them any safer. Our children face numerous challenges, including drugs, violence, and bullying.

As a result, many schools have hired police officers to patrol the hallways and to act as liaisons with students. Part of their job is to get to know the students—to help students feel comfortable talking with the officers when help was needed.

A Cop Who Really Cared

Character First received a phone call one day from Sgt. Clarence Powers, a community relations officer with the police department who was assigned to the Oklahoma City Public Schools. His job was to help make the schools safe and to develop a rapport with the students.

Sgt. Powers saw a disturbing trend. When he had first started working for the police department, young people tended to be 16-18 years old before they were caught committing crimes. Although they were still juveniles, many of them were old enough to be considered adults. As the years went by, students as young as 10-12 were caught breaking the law.

This deeply concerned Sgt. Powers. He knew if these children kept making the same choices, by the age of 18 they would have made so many bad decisions that their options for a successful life would be very limited.

Sgt. Powers mentioned his concerns to the Oklahoma County District Attorney, Wes Lane, who knew that Character First was helping organizations around the world. At his suggestion, Sgt. Powers contacted us, and together we started the process of building a program that could be used in public schools.

Before consideration by a school system, we had to present a complete program for the entire nine-month school year. After developing a teaching plan, we scheduled a meeting with the superintendant of Oklahoma City Public Schools, anticipating a lengthy process to have our character program approved.

Before our meeting ended, however, we were approved to teach Character First as a pilot project in eight Oklahoma City schools. Within three years, we were teaching character in 40 schools. Now more than a decade later, Character First is still being taught in some of the original eight schools. Over the years, we have worked in 60 of the 63 elementary schools in the Oklahoma City Public Schools system.

Sometimes, it is hard to measure the impact that Character First has on a particular organization. We can't always put numbers on how character training improves an environment or the lives of people. However, we can rely on the judgment and experience of the qualified professionals who work with those organizations—in this instance, the teachers and principals who interact with students on a daily basis and have watched the progress of character training in their schools.

One year after Character First was used in the Oklahoma City Public Schools, a survey was taken to measure its effectiveness. Four questions were asked of teachers and principals:

- **"Did students show an increased knowledge of character?"** Ninety percent of teachers responded "Yes," and 88 percent of principals agreed with them.

- **"Has character training improved your relationships with students?"** Sixty-eight percent of teachers and 75 percent of principals answered "Yes."

- **"Have you noticed a decrease in discipline problems since Character First was introduced in the school?"** Forty-seven percent of teachers and 50 percent of principals said "Yes."

- **"Have you seen evidence that students are applying character training?"** Sixty-eight percent of teachers and 75 percent of principals said they had watched students apply the character qualities in real-life situations.

Once we were able to implement Character First at Oklahoma City Public Schools, we were accepted into schools across the country. We have received numerous positive evaluations from teachers around the world.

"The materials are of great quality and very easy to implement. As a first- and now second-grade teacher, I believe the curriculum plants seeds and goals for the students to recognize and attain."

"If we continue to implement this material, I foresee some changes from both the teachers and students. Teachers will be able to communicate with students, and the students will get along better with their peers and teachers. All students need to be educated and to understand that character education is part of their everyday lives—starting from home, to school, to applying what they have learned into their jobs. They will become a better person if they put to practice what they are learning from this curriculum. I let them know on a daily basis the importance—that Character Education will impact their personality and lives from now on until they die."

"Let me just say that I not only use Character First at school, but also at home with my own children. The tool has many benefits and should be taught in every school in America."

Topeka Public Schools

Topeka, Kansas, was feeling the impact of poor character throughout the entire community. A corruption scandal rocked the city government. Absenteeism, low test scores, and on-campus bullying plagued the schools. The issue of character became important to the entire city as the citizens struggled to deal with these issues.

At the same time, the United States federal government began offering grants for character educational initiatives. City leaders in Topeka, eager to change the culture of their city, applied for grant money. The city was awarded a grant and chose to use the bulk of the funds to instill character in public schools.

Character First worked closely with the school district to create and implement character training, based on the model that had worked so well for Oklahoma City Public Schools. The training was established in 32 schools over a four-year period.

In addition, the grant money allowed the school system to hire an independent, outside company to measure the effectiveness of character training. The schools were measured in eight areas—including academic achievement, generosity, parent involvement, and quality of life. It also surveyed the schools regarding responsibility, self-confidence, truth, and work ethic. At the end of the study, the numbers were clear. Schools that received the most character training saw the greatest improvement in all of these areas. Two other findings were significant:

- **Character training in middle schools is particularly important.** For many students, grades 6-8 are often chaotic and challenging. "Middle school in North America carries with it associations of personal and emotional difficulty," states Wikipedia. "Physical and hormonal changes that accompany adolescence are exacerbated by newfound self-consciousness, social pressures, and the desire for conformity and identity." The improvements made by teaching Character First to this age group reinforce the impact of good character.

- **Students' grades did not drop.** Teaching character did not prevent the students from doing their normal class work. In fact, character training does not need to impact class time at all. When character training is fully integrated into a school, teachers will teach character by example and will praise for character daily. This improves the culture in schools, without diverting class time.

> *Character First can change our schools.*
> *It can change our homes.*
> *It can change our businesses.*
> *Character First can change our world.*

CHAPTER 16

CHARACTER FIRST AROUND THE GLOBE

Character First is now used in over 34 countries, and all or parts of the materials have been translated into at least 12 languages. These represent an incredibly broad range of cultures.

Many people initially expressed concern that Character First would not work in their countries. They thought our success was due to the culture of the United States. At first, I had the same concern, but that has not been a limiting factor. Character First has been well received by participants in all these countries, and it has a powerful, positive impact wherever it is used.

Character First has been successful because it crosses all racial, gender, and geographic lines. It doesn't matter how old you are, what you look like, where you live, or how you choose to worship. If you apply the principles of good character, you will begin making better decisions that foster success.

The rapid growth of Character First and its impact on a diverse group of companies, organizations, and institutions should not have been a surprise to anyone. Character First is transformational because it is based on human nature and meets universal needs. It helps people fulfill their natural desire to please those they respect—and to receive recognition and appreciation from them.

F. X. Morales & Associates— Monterrey, Mexico

As I recall, the first business outside the United States to use Character First was F.X. Morales & Associates (FXM) in Monterrey, Mexico. FXM represents and distributes premium-quality food products and ingredients in Mexico and has stressed strong values ever since it was founded in 1988. As the company grew, however, founder Xavier Morales decided character would have to be formally taught if they hoped to maintain their core values.

Mr. Morales attended a seminar we conducted in Dallas, Texas, in the early 1990s. I had the privilege of meeting him at the seminar and explaining the difference character training had made in many organizations. After the seminar, Mr. Morales returned to Monterrey and incorporated Character First into his company—where it continues to make a difference to this day.

Character training has helped FXM become one of the largest independent food distributors in Mexico. It has simplified transmitting their business values to customers, suppliers, and new employees. The monthly meetings also help all employees understand what is expected of them, which is reflected in the way they do business. FXM employees are interested in reinforcing their character and have learned how to praise others for good character. This transmits FXM's business philosophy to others and has become an important part of its culture.

The employees of F.X. Morales say it best:

> *"Character First has allowed us to have a starting point to dialogue about character qualities— and their importance, reach, and implementation—*

not only in our working relations, but in our entire life experience."

"This program stimulates us to develop the most important part of the human being, while making us confront ourselves (and our weaknesses)... and to develop a firm character that can help us become better persons, and consequently, better employees. So the objective of Character First is to develop the potential of the employees so they can become better people, and thus have an impact on the society we are living in."

"We don't realize the importance of character in our lives until we face difficulties, crisis, and adversity. But if we work on them, we will see positive results, and the character qualities will let us respond to these moments in different ways."

In 2008, I was asked to lead a seminar for another organization in Monterrey. While in town, I visited FXM and heard reports from their management and employees about the positive impact Character First has had on the company. I also had the privilege of attending the company's quarterly training session and speaking at its 20th anniversary celebration. They continue to use Character First and see it as a major benefit to their employees—and a contributing factor to their success, including the amazing growth and expansion of their product line.

Evento Integral—Mexico City

Francisco and Margarita Cabrera are a husband-and-wife team who lead Evento Integral, a world-class producer of major events and conferences in Mexico City. The company provides and sets up audio-visual equipment, and supplies translation services.

The Cabreras worked together in the company, but the pressures of work, marriage, and unresolved conflict created difficulties. They eventually went through the process of divorce but continued working together—and spent the next 14 years as Evento Integral co-workers who lived separate lives outside of the business.

Getting Personal

Then their daughter Itzel, who was studying in the United States, heard about Character First. Itzel felt it could help her family's company, but she especially hoped it would help her parents' relationship. She explained Character First to her parents and told them why she thought it was important they attend training. Both parents were interested, but only Margarita took the time to attend.

After Margarita returned from Character First training, Francisco saw positive changes in her life and decided he should also attend the training. As the Cabreras applied what they had learned, the issues that caused their marriage to fail melted away. They were able to forgive each other and restore their relationship, and eventually they decided to remarry.

As Francisco and Margarita prepared for the ceremony, they discovered the divorce-court judge had never filed their divorce papers. The couple had lived apart for more than a decade, not realizing they were still legally husband and wife.

"We've been married 39 years," said Francisco, "including a 14-year vacation."

Breaking New Ground

Once the Cabreras experienced the change that character training could bring, they were passionate about using it in their company, even though many of the materials were not yet available in Spanish. Evento Integral's first attempts at Character First were enthusiastic but had limited impact; a key reason was they didn't have a clear idea of how to implement character training in a practical way. After attending additional training seminars, the Cabreras began praising for character, holding employee meetings, and implementing application sessions—and they began seeing positive results.

Character eventually became ingrained in the culture of Evento Integral. It has helped families be successful, improved workplace relationships, improved morale, and inspired employees to constantly strive for excellence. Monica Garcia, an Evento Integral employee, stated, "Character First has been the high standard that I want to reach every day."

One unique thing about Evento Integral's implementation of Character First is the company encourages family members to attend the monthly employee meetings. Spouses and children of employees give testimonies about how character training has impacted their families, and many of them tell how it helped restore their relationships. The company views this as the most valuable result of adopting Character First.

The Cabreras were encouraged by the results and wanted other families and organizations to receive the benefits of character training. To accomplish this, Evento Integral sponsored the translation and production of additional Character First materials. It also organized and sponsored the first Character First seminar in Mexico City. Over 100 businesses came to the first conference. The training was so well received that additional conferences were held in Mexico, and seminars were requested in Guatemala, Costa Rica, and other Latin American countries.

> *"Before Character First arrived in my life, I felt I was indispensable to the company and that they were not worthy of me. I was angry at my authorities for not adopting my plans and ideas. This anger was so intense that I had high blood pressure, which was complicated with diabetes.*
>
> *Character First training helped me learn to yield my rights and personal expectations when appropriate and develop a desire to serve. I began to understand that humility is better than pride and to develop meekness.*
>
> *I also learned to respect and honor my authorities and be more flexible. I learned how to make an appeal when there is a risk of damage to the image of the company or my authorities, and I have learned how to interact in a more positive way with clients and suppliers.*
>
> *I now have a good relationship and respect for my authorities and coworkers."*
>
> Oralia Vertiz
> Evento Integral employee

The Cabreras have become more than enthusiastic supporters of Character First. They have become the Character First representatives for Mexico and have a vision for bringing character training to businesses, schools, and prisons throughout Latin America.

Everlight Chemical Industrial Corporation—Taipei, Taiwan

Character First was invited to train businesses in Taipei, Taiwan. In spite of my belief that character is a universal need and not a cultural issue, I worried that the problems in Asia would be so different that Character First would not work there. My friends in Taipei assured me that it would work even with the language barrier, but I still could not shake my concerns.

Out of desperation, I subscribed to the English version of the *China Times*. I read the newspaper for several months before we left and was amazed that the problems and difficulties it reported were the same as in any newspaper in a major U.S. city. This reassured me that character issues were the same around the world. With my confidence renewed, we scheduled and conducted the first of many Character First seminars in Taiwan.

A Revelation in Taiwan

The first major company in Taiwan to use Character First was Everlight Chemical Industrial Corporation, the country's dye industry leader. Everlight's founder and Chairman of the Board, Ding-Chuan Chen, had been teaching integrity and character inside his company since founding it in 1972.

Mr. Chen learned about the Character First training that was scheduled for September 1997 in Taiwan. He immediately recognized that the training would help reinforce Everlight's management philosophy: "The pursuit of progress and innovation, the stimulation of individual potential, and contribution to the quality of life."

Mr. Chen attended the training and brought 60 managers from Everlight. To his team, the three-day seminar was a revelation—and within four months, Everlight was implementing Character First company-wide.

Getting Started at Everlight

Everlight began by translating Character First materials into Chinese for its employees to read and discuss. It also began to praise for character in monthly meetings, on employees' birthdays, and daily, when anyone saw good character being exhibited. Some departments created a "character mailbox," and people who witnessed good character were encouraged to jot it down and drop it in the box. The boxes were opened during monthly meetings, and the character reports were shared with all of the employees. After the meetings, some departments also documented key points on cards that employees can wear around their necks.

Everlight communicated the character qualities it expected in several ways, including publishing a quarterly magazine, using character cards and posters, and posting real-life examples of good character on the company website. The company began holding an annual celebration, with booths for its employees to play character games. Everlight changed its employee evaluation to include character as 20 percent of every individual's performance review. During job interviews, applicants were now required to answer questions about character.

Thirteen years later, Character First continues to be an integral part of the company. It has become a platform to help its employees reach their full potential, increase their families' sense of worth, and impact their communities.

Beyond Everlight

Mr. Chen's commitment to character training has grown beyond the implementation at Everlight—he believes character is essential for his community and Taiwan as a whole.

In December 1998, he assumed the role of Chairman of the Board of the Pei Ji Educational Foundation, with the goal of promoting character education throughout Taiwan. With the foundation, Mr. Chen has introduced character training to elementary schools throughout Taiwan and launched a summer camp near the Everlight factory, where many Everlight employees volunteer to help students learn character.

Taiwan was just the beginning of Character First's influence in Asia. We have now conducted seminars in Korea, Singapore, Indonesia, Malaysia, Mongolia, Philippines, Hong Kong, Macau, and China.

The Costa Group— Victoria, Australia

A Disappointing Introduction

Several years ago, I met with business leaders in Perth, Australia and explained the concept of praising employees and co-workers for good character. The business leaders said that would not work in Australia. They told me that Australians never praise a person directly. They frequently insult each other in a good-natured way and receive that as a compliment. For instance, instead of saying "You are a valued employee," a supervisor might say, "You are a dirty dog." The fact that you recognize and speak to the person is received as praise.

The first introduction of Character First to Australia was a complete disappointment. A year later, however, a series of events began to culminate that gave Character First another opportunity.

History of Excellence

The Costa Group is family-owned. In four generations, they have grown from a small family business to a company with over 8,000 employees across 48 locations in Australia and have annual revenues that exceed $800 million.

The Costa Group is one of Australia's largest privately owned companies and is the largest privately owned company in the food industry. The Costa Group provides fresh produce to Australian supermarket chains from an extensive network of farming operations, wholesale outlets, export and import offices, and warehouses and distribution centers. When I say fresh, I mean fresh. In many parts of the world, it is not uncommon for fruits or vegetables—especially potatoes—to sit in a warehouse for months before people have the chance to buy them. After Costa harvests vegetables or fruits, they reach a bin at the grocery store within days, sometimes within 24 hours.

Costa has always focused on values and character. When they were a small company, the family easily modeled character for the entire workforce. But as the third and forth generations of the family transformed it into a network of thousands of people in national and international operations, it became challenging for these family values to be understood and applied by all of the employees.

In the mid 1990s, Chairman Frank Costa began searching for a way he could teach every employee the values and behaviors he wanted reflected in the company. He reviewed many "programs" but wasn't satisfied that any of them would produce the results he wanted. He doubted they could be applied in the Australian culture, where people tend to be cynical of any type of employee training or personal recognition.

Then Mr. Costa learned about Character First, and in 1998 he sent a senior executive to Oklahoma to attend a three-day, Character First seminar. After the training, the executive exclaimed, "This is exactly what we need! I am excited to go back to Australia and begin Character First in our company."

Common Experience

Character First addresses fundamental issues and touches people at a very deep level. We have many committed and enthusiastic trainers. People cannot attend one of our seminars without seeing the incredible value that character training offers, and this makes them want to change the core values of their organizations immediately.

Early Challenges

I didn't know it at the time, but the senior executive had faced resistance even before he left Australia. There was a strong "push-back" within Costa, and many employees were concerned that Character First was another Employee of the Month program. These had already been tried at Costa—and failed. When the senior executive returned and passionately detailed the differences between Character First and the programs they had already tried, Costa management committed to implement character training. However, it was harder to get middle management and the rest of the workforce to buy in.

Fortunately, the Costa brothers—Frank, Anthony, Kevin, and Robert—had been teaching and modeling character for years. They had developed an excellent reputation in the Australian fresh-produce industry for honesty and fairness—values that had always been non-negotiable for them. When they realized their need for formal training from Character First to be implemented throughout Costa, it helped that our ideas were consistent with what their family had been doing for generations.

The challenges that Costa faced were the same that arise in virtually every organization that shifts from a culture of criticism to a culture of praise. As at hundreds of other companies around the world, managers at Costa posed challenging questions for us:

- "How do you get everyone to buy in?"
- "How long will it take to change the culture?"
- "Do I really have to have meetings once a month?"
- "How can we afford that much employee down-time?"

In addition to those initial reactions, Costa discovered the common problem that many of their supervisors were naturally afraid of speaking in public. They also saw that when supervisors began to emphasize character traits, there was a tendency by some employees to think these expectations required "perfection" in the workplace. This put a significant amount of pressure on the entire workforce in a short period of time.

Surprising Benefits

Although Costa was quite concerned about these challenges, in reality they were common issues that Character First is well accustomed to helping organizations address. One of our recommendations was that Costa provide public-speaking training for its supervisors. In addition to giving supervisors more confidence in dealing with people, Costa reaped benefits it did not expect—supervisors began to have higher-quality interactions with customers.

Character First also provided Costa the framework to teach and reinforce the family values it cherished. It has allowed Frank Costa to educate his employees so that they consistently demonstrate good character throughout his family's organization.

Once Costa was known for emphasizing character, they began to attract employees who understood the importance of character and wanted to work in a character-rich environment. This stabilized the workforce, reduced personnel problems, and decreased the costs of hiring new employees. Character training also expanded Costa's client base. Customers wanted to do business with a company that treated them with virtue, honor, and sincerity.

Character First has helped Costa develop a reputation for consistently practicing good behavior. It did not give mere lip service by placing a poster on the wall and hoping its employees would do the right thing. It taught, modeled, and reinforced character in the workplace. This forced employees at every level to consider their actions carefully and has enabled Costa to establish a consistent business model for recruiting, training, and retaining employees across the entire organization.

In addition, Costa has noticed Character First created a "ripple effect" on the families of people who come in contact with the organization. Costa regularly hears stories of how character training has been taken into the homes of its employees and enhanced their lives.

At Costa, Character First has become more than a monthly meeting or a training and development initiative. It has become a genuine part of the organization and has created an expectation of character from every member of the company. It is in the DNA of the organization.

> *"I think Character First is fantastic. It may not mean as much to people as what Simon and Frank would like it to mean, but you can't solve all the problems with one monthly meeting... . Character First means different things to different people, but more than anything else it sets us apart ... it makes our company different ... and I think it's brilliant that so many of the rank-and-file workers—who some might consider to be 'nobodies'—are recognized by their peers and their bosses."*
>
> Gary Meadows
> Costa employee[12]

China

Several years ago, the Chinese government invited Character First to conduct a seminar in Beijing. Since we didn't know how well we would be received, we booked a small venue. As the date approached, we were forced to upgrade to a larger venue twice to accommodate the amount of interest. Character First was enthusiastically embraced, and we were invited to meet with officials from major universities and powerful businesses.

Our next Chinese classroom was in Shanghai, where we taught another well-attended and well-received workshop. The day after the seminar, we were invited to a large company whose executives had attended the training. When we arrived, we were greeted with huge banners that displayed the 49 character qualities and their definitions, translated into Chinese, hanging in conspicuous places throughout the company. The company had seen the need for Character First and wasted no time in getting started—they had all the banners translated, manufactured, and in place within 24 hours.

Other companies also showed interest in using character training to build a solid foundation for their employees. Today, we have Character First offices in Hong Kong and Shanghai to train business executives.

Malaysia

The Malaysian government invited Character First to be a presenter at the International Conference on Families in Kuala Lumpur in October 2001. The Secretary of the National Population and Family Development Board was so impressed with Character First that she traveled to Oklahoma City to see how Character First could help the families in all of Malaysia.

She was not the only member of the Malaysian government to see the importance of Character First. "This program is exactly what we need for our country," commented another government official.

Africa

Character First recently authorized trainers in South Africa. Character training has been received enthusiastically and has spread to nearby countries. In Rwanda, President Paul Kagame has expressed an interest in Character First and believes it can be a major component of leadership development programs for current and future leaders.

CHAPTER 17

HIRING FOR CHARACTER

In *Good To Great,* best-selling author Jim Collins wrote of the importance of getting "the right people on the bus" and "the wrong people off the bus."[13] Hiring the right people is one of the most critical processes in any organization.

Rapid growth, a need to meet customer demands, and many other pressures can push us to make employment decisions without fully considering the consequences. Every employee impacts productivity, morale, profits, and customer service. We should approach every hiring decision with care, whether we are hiring a temporary employee, a laborer, an assistant, or a top-level manager.

New Times Bring New Challenges

Hiring a person of character wasn't always as difficult as it is today. There is a railroad track that runs past Kimray's plant. One hot summer day in the late 1950s, a young man who had just finished high school was walking down the tracks to Oklahoma City to find a job. As he passed our plant, he saw a man standing in the shade of the garage door, and they waved to each other. The young man walked over to enjoy a respite from the sun and began to chat. When asked where he was

going and what he was doing, the young man said he was going to town to find a job. It just happened that the man in the
doorway was the plant manager, and he replied, "Why don't
you work here?" The young man accepted the offer on the
spot, eventually was promoted to plant manager himself, and
worked for Kimray until he retired.

This probably would not happen today. About 50 percent
of the job applicants who walk in the front door of Kimray
cannot pass a drug/alcohol test. Illegal drug use and alcohol
abuse involve character issues that cripple companies.

According to the American Council for Drug Education,
more than 70 percent of substance abusers hold jobs. They
don't have to indulge on the job to have a negative impact
on the workplace. Compared to their non-abusing co-workers,
substance abusers are 33 percent less productive, 10 times
more likely to miss work, and five times more likely to file a
workers' compensation claim. They are nearly four times more
likely to be involved in on-the-job accidents and five times
more likely to injure themselves or others in the process.[14]

Kimray owned a cast and ductile iron foundry for about
five years. One day a supervisor caught his hand in the molding
machine. We took him to the hospital for treatment, and in
accordance with our policy for employees involved in accidents,
he was tested for illegal drugs and alcohol. The test showed he
was legally drunk. We were surprised, because he wasn't acting
abnormally; but we later learned why we didn't recognize his
drunkenness: we probably had never seen him sober.

The Wrong Shortcuts Can Lead to Failure

The pressure to shortcut established hiring processes and
to ignore internal warnings can be intense. Early in my career,
our company was in a critical position. Our sales had expanded
rapidly, and we had purchased expensive machines and raw

materials, but our backlog of orders continued to grow. We hired the few unskilled workers who were available and began to train them. Even so, our backlog of orders increased. Our failure to make timely deliveries opened the door for our competition to solicit business that had historically been ours.

During those critical years, we failed to be conscientious in hiring. As a result, instead of increasing productivity, we watched those figures plummet. At the same time, tardiness, absenteeism, theft, accidents, and workers' compensation costs all climbed. And as you can imagine, our personnel problems increased dramatically. Looking back, I believe it would have been better to restrict our growth than to hire without proper procedures and suffer the repercussions.

Hiring for Character, First

Exactly how important is character when hiring? Is character more important than skill, or is skill more important than character? Where is the balance? Do you have to choose between character and skill, or is it possible for a person to have both skill and character?

"In determining 'the right people,'" observed Jim Collins, "the good-to-great companies placed greater weight on character attributes than on specific educational background, practical skills, specialized knowledge, or work experience."[15] To have a great company, character must be the most important criteria in the hiring process.

Kimray needed to establish hiring procedures that would enable us to hire the people best-suited for the organization—in good times and bad. If our organization was to be noted for a culture of character, we had to make hiring decisions based on the character of every prospective employee.

Kimray's typical employment application wasn't sufficient. It requested only personal information such as name, Social

Security number, address, type of employment sought, education, special training or skills, former employers, and references. Frequently, when Kimray contacted an applicant's previous employers, they would only verify employment and eligibility for rehiring. When Kimray contacted the applicant's references, we usually heard a good report—because the applicant had carefully selected those references. The bottom line is that our employment application was skill-based and gave us little insight into the character of the prospective employee.

So we asked ourselves two questions:

- Is it possible to discern the character of an individual in the hiring process?
- Is it legal to ask the kind of questions that might reveal the character of future employees?

Is It Possible?

The answer to our first question was "Yes"—if we could ask questions about past behavior. The best predictor of an individual's character is revealed by past responses to varying situations, especially difficult ones.

> *I have but one lamp by which my feet are*
> *guided, and that is the lamp of experience.*
> *I know no other way of judging the future*
> *but by the past.* Patrick Henry

We needed something that would help us discover who people really were—their inner motivations and core values. We decided to create an addendum to our application that would guide us during interviews. It contained character-based questions that would help us discern the specific qualities and overall character of a prospective employee.

A Little Digging

When I was a boy working in my grandmother's garden, at harvest time we didn't know how many potatoes were in the ground without doing a little digging. The same is true of character. You can't determine a person's character without a little digging.

Obviously, we cannot discuss or ask questions about all possible character qualities during the interview process. Therefore, we chose a few primary character qualities that we could reasonably expect to discuss in an interview. We specifically address punctuality, orderliness, truthfulness, loyalty, contentment, obedience, forgiveness, tolerance, and humility.

For example, on the topic of punctuality, at Kimray we typically ask whether the applicant's previous supervisors would say the person was consistently on time, and how previous employers would rate the applicant's attendance. Depending on their answers, we often ask follow-up questions to give further insight into who the applicants are. (For more examples of interview questions, see *Appendix B*.)

Is It Legal?

When our attorneys first reviewed our character addendum, their answer to our second question was "No"—which is the typical response from good, conservative lawyers to any bold ideas. They felt it might violate the law to ask any questions that were not pertinent to the job or the performance of the employee.

We explained to our attorneys that employees' character is extremely important to their jobs. Every organization has good reasons to know the character of its employees. We provided several examples to help our lawyers fully understand how character truly is pertinent to the job:

- **Trustworthiness.** If you were hiring a teller at a bank, would it be important to know if the person is trustworthy? Of course. Would it be wise to ask questions to determine their trustworthiness? Certainly.

- **Punctuality.** In manufacturing plants, there are shifts where one employee replaces another. If the relieving employee is late, it places a hardship on the employee who has already worked a full shift. In some cases, tardiness can disrupt the process and cause considerable loss.

- **Safety.** Employers have a duty to provide a safe workplace for all of their employees, and they must know the character of everyone who works for them to fulfill that duty. Unresolved anger and bitterness (both character issues) are major problems in the workplace today. Instead of harboring grudges and holding onto old resentments, good character is forgiving and tolerant. Studies have shown that murder is the second-leading cause of death of women in the workplace, and the third-leading cause of death of men in the workplace.[16] The act of one employee murdering another has become so prevalent it has been nicknamed "going postal." Exercise caution in hiring or suffer potentially damaging consequences in the future.

- **Orderliness and Obedience.** For a company to be competitive, everything and every person must work together to accomplish tasks in the most efficient manner. This requires orderliness and the willingness to follow instructions and procedures.

After our explanation and discussion about how character was pertinent and required to do the job effectively, the attorneys agreed that the questions and follow-up discussion could be legal, and they could make a case and defend us if necessary.

Since expanding our employment application two decades ago to include character, we have never been legally challenged. Even so, my advice is that you discuss your employment application with your legal counsel before implementing a change.

Be Creative

It helps to be creative when trying to discern a person's true character. Thomas Edison was an ingenious entrepreneur. He had 1,093 U.S. patents, a record that still stands today. He employed and worked with a team of engineers and inventors. The story is told that when Edison was considering a new employee, he would take him to lunch and order soup for the two of them. When the soup arrived, he would watch the prospect. If the prospect salted his soup before tasting it, it signaled that he acted on assumptions without testing them first—and so Edison would not hire him.

Some people may look at this example and ask, "What does salting soup have to do with engineering?" Edison thought like a true engineer, and he believed all employees should do the same. That meant constantly questioning and testing their environment—and never assuming any facts they had not proven. Edison knew that if one of his employees made assumptions during the course of his workday, it could spell the difference between a new invention that could change the world and failure.

A friend of mine owned rental houses and had a history of good tenants and few problems. He said the key to his success was observing a prospective renter's car after the interview. If the car was full of trash and in obvious disrepair, my friend would not rent to him or her. He felt people who would not take care of their own property wouldn't take care of rental property.

Count the Cost

It is expensive to hire a new employee. The turnover costs for an employee can be 75-150 percent of his or her annual salary[17]. It may take a little more time and money to hire a person of good character, but it is worth it. If you hire a thief who knows how to use a computer, he may use it to steal from you. But if you train a person of character to use a computer, she will use it to benefit the organization. Does your company have a process for hiring that considers the character of its applicants?

A few sample questions from Kimray's application are included in *Appendix B*. These questions have worked for us, but you must rely on the advice of your professionals to ensure they fit your needs and are appropriate for your organization. The questions should cause a prospect to think and respond. Her answers will give you the opportunity to follow up with additional questions and discussion. Remember, you are trying to discover the core values of the prospect that may be different from her reputation. You want to know who she *really* is—her character.

I know of only three ways to transform the culture of your organization into a culture of character. One is to help those in the company build good character. Another is to hire people of good character. The third is to terminate those with bad character who refuse to change. Each is vital to the health of your organization, and you must do all three. But it is easier to hire people with good character than to change their character after they are hired.

If you want a company with a culture of character and employees known for their character, you must hire for character. There is no other way, and there are no shortcuts.

> *Hire for character—train for skills.*

CHAPTER 18

CORRECTING FOR CHARACTER

A supervisor's most-dreaded responsibility may be dealing with personnel problems. Bad attitudes, tardiness, gossip, poor attendance, lying, stealing, negligence, preventable accidents, and secret agendas, are all manifestations of poor character.

Think about the last time you had to fire an employee. Why was he fired? Was it for a lack of skills, or was it due to a character issue? I have asked hundreds of CEOs and business leaders this question, and their answers are the same. The last time they had to fire anyone was because of a character issue. Unfortunately, firing usually occurs only after repeated problems with an employee. A leader may spend many hours dealing with a problem-employee, and even then, the issues may never be resolved.

Surveys reveal that leaders spend between 30 percent[18] and 42 percent[19] of their time trying to resolve conflicts. If you calculate all the time spent on all character-related problems, this can jump to 70-80 percent. Employees with poor character can quickly monopolize a supervisor's time and distract her from focusing on the issues that can turn your company from good to great.

No one is perfect. Every manager will eventually have to correct an employee. The issue is not *if* you will have to provide correction—but *when*. You need to be prepared so that it is done in a way that is best for the individual and the company.

Proper correction resolves problems quickly, provides instruction, leads to repentance, restores relationships, and promotes positive behavior changes that prevent or reduce future problems. Leaders will reap huge dividends if they correct properly. It also gives supervisors additional time to focus on the real issues of the company.

I could not, in good conscience, tell a leader she has to learn one more leadership skill and add Character First to her list of daily activities without knowing the payoff was worth the effort. If she were to reduce her personnel problems by just 20 percent, she would have over an hour a day to invest in employees, herself, and the organization. Implementing Character First, including learning how to correct properly, can recover lost time, increase morale and productivity, and strengthen the culture of your company.

The Foundation

The foundation for proper and meaningful correction is a right relationship between your employees and you. You should begin laying the foundation for correction when employees are hired or when you become their supervisor. Hopefully, you have done this long before correction is needed. Wrong attitudes, actions, and words—all manifestations of bad character— demonstrate that relationships are damaged. The primary goal of correction is to restore these damaged relationships.

Some managers believe they need to distance themselves from their employees and do not become involved in their lives. They try to maintain control by being distant. This is wrong and doesn't work.

If you have previously failed to establish an appropriate relationship with every employee on your team, you can begin today. To develop proper relationships, a leader must establish standards of behavior and define expectations. It may take longer because you have to correct established patterns, break old habits, and build new ones, but you can do it.

Expectations

We have many good leaders at Kimray. One leader, Charlie, was especially effective at orienting new employees. He would explain the functions of each job in detail, so that everyone knew what they were required to do. Charlie also stated his expectations regarding breaks, attendance, horseplay, cursing, attire, and diligence. If anyone was unable to meet his requirements, there might be an opportunity for training; but ultimately, an individual's consistent failure could result in termination. His employees knew what he expected and the consequences of failure.

The very first time an employee was late, Charlie would take him or her aside and bluntly ask, "Do you want this job? Do you want to work? If you do, you need to show me by being here on time and ready to work. If you don't want to work, tell me now. We will cut you a check, and you can look for a job elsewhere." He did not wait until the second or third time. He established expectations from the start, was consistent in defining expectations, and addressed problems immediately when they arose.

When our son Thomas was 16 years old, he worked for Charlie one summer. Some employees may have thought Thomas would get special treatment because he was my son. On Thomas' second day at work, however, Charlie pulled him aside and told him, "I know who you are, and I know who your daddy is. You need to understand that because of who you are, you will be expected to work harder than anyone else. If you aren't willing to do that, then you need to work somewhere else." My son immediately knew who his boss was and what was expected of him.

> *Expectations are important. Set them early, set them high, and give your employees the tools to succeed.*

Kimray also needed to translate its expectations into company policies that every employee could understand. We wanted policies based on the standard of good character—the forty-nine character qualities and their definitions from Character First. Our Employee Handbook gives employees not only an overall vision for our company, but also a detailed explanation of topics including ethics, performance evaluations, correction, job responsibility, drug testing, personal appearance, use of electronic devices, workers' compensation insurance, and our 401(k) retirement/profit sharing plan and other benefits. In addition, praising for character, using character definitions, illustrations, and benefits establishes and communicates a standard and an expectation of good character.

Be An Example

I remember seeing the following quote on a marquee: "What you are doing speaks so loudly that I can't hear what you are saying." John Maxwell said it a little differently: "People do what people see."[20] The bottom line is that our actions speak louder than our words.

This places a high expectation on leaders. You cannot expect your employees to be punctual if you are not. You cannot expect your employees to be patient with customers if you are not. You cannot expect your employees to take responsibility for their actions if you don't take responsibility for yours.

Does this mean that you have to be perfect? Absolutely not. Not even your harshest critics expect you to be faultless. What is expected—and what many leaders have difficulty doing—is admitting when they are wrong, asking forgiveness, and changing their behavior. Simple—but not easy. One of the most difficult things you will do as a leader is admit when you are wrong. And it's even harder to take ownership of your actions and ask for forgiveness.

Many leaders think admitting an error is a sign of weakness and undermines respect. But that is simply not true. Own your actions, take responsibility for your mistakes, and seek forgiveness when required. This will build respect and loyalty.

> *Men are respectable only as they respect.*
> Emerson

Being held strictly accountable for our actions is a strong motivator to change. If you are committed to admitting when you are wrong and seeking forgiveness, you will have a tremendous sense of accountability. This can motivate you to change and build good character.

I specifically remember one executive meeting at Kimray when I got very upset. I responded with angry words, angry looks, and angry responses. Several people left the meeting confused and hurt. After I calmed down, I knew I needed to ask forgiveness of everyone involved. Saying only "I'm sorry" is ineffective and insincere. Instead, I reflected on how my behavior had made each person feel.

"I was wrong to get angry in our meeting," I confessed to them. "I know it is difficult to feel safe and say what is on your mind when you risk getting an angry response from me. Will you forgive me?" Each person graciously forgave me, and I worked in subsequent meetings to restore the level of trust I had enjoyed before.

Speak when you are angry and you'll
make the best speech you'll ever regret.
Lawrence J. Peter
Letter to Congress, April 30, 1789

Your walk walks and your talk talks,
but your walk talks louder than your talk talks.

Demonstrate True Concern

No one cares how much you know,
until they know how much you care.
Theodore Roosevelt

As leaders, we frequently try to lead by demonstrating how much knowledge we have accumulated. We can feel pressure to prove that we have earned our positions, and this creates problems. How can we earn the right to be heard? We must first have concern for the employees, their families, their health, their hobbies, and their faith. It is difficult to have true concern for people we don't know.

Most of my business career was in sales. (Isn't every businessperson in sales?) When calling on a customer for the first time, I knew very little about her. Hopefully, during the meeting I would learn a few personal facts. Is she married? Does she have children? How long has she been in her current position? What are her hobbies? These facts are considered public information, so it's socially acceptable to ask the questions.

It can be difficult to remember this information, yet few things demonstrate the importance of a customer more than recalling personal facts in subsequent meetings. Good salesmen either have a knack for remembering or have a good contact management system. With my failing memory, I need help. I started with a Rolodex, graduated to a Palm Pilot, and now use an iPhone.

If we go to such lengths to demonstrate the importance of a customer, why would we do anything less for our employees? Depending on how many individuals you supervise, you may or may not need a contact manager. Even if you only have one or two employees, you need to be purposeful about talking with them to discover public information. This demonstrates true concern.

Engage them in conversation by asking questions, but don't violate their privacy. Only ask questions you would ask someone you have just met. For example:

- "What are your hobbies?"
- "What do you like to do on weekends?"
- "Are you married?"
- "What is your spouse's name?"
- "Do you have children?"
- "How old are they?"
- "Where do they go to school?"
- "What is your favorite sport?"
- "How long have you been with the company?"

After you ask a question, let the employee talk. This may be the most difficult part. Listening is a skill few of us have mastered.

> *It takes a great man to make a good listener.* Arthur Helps

If you need help remembering details, return to your office and enter the information into your contact program. This is not rocket science. Even so, some leaders fail to understand the importance of discovering public information or don't know the best way to gather it.

I remember one leader who approached an employee, pulled out a notebook, and began asking questions, "How long have you worked here?" Then he wrote the answer in his notebook. He then asked, "What is your wife's name?" and wrote down the answer in front of the employee. The supervisor is to be commended for seeking to learn more about his employees, but I doubt that employee felt honored. Remember, the best way to show interest and true concern is to ask questions and listen. Talk about your employees' interests rather than your own.

As you develop a relationship, the discussions may touch on more private information. Employees may feel comfortable discussing family illnesses, children, or difficult personal situations. When employees share private information with you, they are demonstrating an unusual level of trust. Don't violate their trust—keep the information confidential, and share it only when given permission.

Act Quickly

Keep in mind that the goal of correction is restoring a broken relationship. You can't sit idly by and hope the problem will resolve itself, because it seldom does. Things may smooth out, but without an appropriate resolution, you will never have the cooperation, authority, or respect you need to be an effective leader.

In addition, as time passes, offenders typically minimize the offense in their mind and begin to justify their actions. The human mind is amazing. Given enough time for self-justification, offenders can even come to the point of believing they are totally innocent. Instead, they believe that you or the rules are at fault. In their mind, they become the victims rather than the offenders.

> *Men count up the faults of those that keep*
> *them waiting.* French Proverb

For many years we have had a company policy dealing with offenses: "Act in the day you hear of it." A large bank has a similar policy of addressing every problem before the close of business on the day it hears of the issue. It is called "The Sundown Rule." The goal is to address every problem the same day we become aware of it, especially personnel problems. Even though you may not have all the facts or know what action to take, notify the offender that you are aware of the problem and are committed to discovering the truth and taking appropriate action.

Nothing is quite as powerful in dealing with an offense as being able to say, "I just heard… ," or, "I just received a report that… ," or, "I just saw… ."

Never Respond In Anger

For many of us, when our employees break a rule or do something wrong, we often feel violated and respond in anger. Many people think, "I don't get angry. I may get upset, I may get irritated, but I'm not angry." Unfortunately, those around you believe you are angry.

I was teaching a men's Sunday school class and asked, "How many of you get angry at least once a day?" Not one man raised his hand. "How about once a week?" Again no hands were raised. "Well then, how many of you get angry at least once a month?" Only a few hands went up. I was flabbergasted.

Then I gave each man 3" x 5" cards for his family members with the following instructions: "Go home and ask your wives and children, 'How can you tell when I am angry, and how often do I get angry?' Don't ask them, 'Do I get angry?' Ask, 'How do you know when I am angry?'"

When the cards were returned, they were filled with behaviors that the family members perceived as anger. These are so insightful and applicable that I've listed more of the quotes in *Appendix C*. Here are a few to highlight my point:

"raises his voice"

"criticizes"

"He puts up a wall."

"My husband says very hurtful things (hurts to the bone)."

"humiliates"

"no patience with children"

"Becomes aggressive."

"Doesn't want to talk about it."

"Really, he is so angry that all he has to do is walk in a room & we feel his anger. We are always *walking on eggshells*."

One wife said that when her husband was mad, he got the vacuum out and swept the carpets. Somewhat jokingly, many of the other wives said they wished their husbands expressed anger in that same way.

> *He who is slow to anger is better than the mighty; and he who rules his spirit better than he who captures a walled city.*
> Proverbs 16:32

You might say, "Tom, that is quite a jump—from kids and spouses, to employees and leaders." Employees are just as perceptive as family members. The key word is "perception." Perception is everything. You may think you are only irritated and not angry, but if your employees perceive you as angry, they will respond as though you are angry. They react to your anger and not to the infraction. This hinders restoration.

> *Keep your temper; nobody else wants it.*
> Unknown

Confront Privately

A major mistake many people make is confronting an offender publicly. Public rebuke is humiliating and can result in bitterness. It robs a person of dignity and leads to disloyalty. This is true of adults and children. Embarrassment can cause us to do and say things that we would not do or say under different circumstances. In addition, when confronted publicly, we have a tendency to defend our reputation rather than consider the wrong we may have committed. Always confront an offender privately. You may need a witness, such as a manager or someone from personnel, but be careful not to confront people in the presence of their co-workers.

Begin by establishing personal responsibility. My natural tendency is to begin by telling the individual what she did wrong. A better way is to let *her* tell *me* by asking, "What did you do?"

Frequently the response will be, "Well, this other person … ."

Calmly repeat the question, "No, what did *you* do?" Continue until the employee finally says, "I did …" and admits what she did. Then clarify the infraction. Repeat what was said and ask if that was what happened.

Appeal to the Conscience

It is important that people acknowledge their wrong behavior. The best way to help them come to that point is to appeal to the conscience—not the will, the emotions, or the physical consequences.

• **Don't appeal to the will.** *"You can do better than that,"* or *"Promise me you will never do that again."* These are usually an effort to elicit a commitment never to repeat the infraction. But if offenders don't believe what they did was wrong—that it only violated your standards, not theirs—the commitment will be hollow and short-lived.

• **Don't appeal to emotions.** *"Don't you know you could have hurt someone?"* or *"How do think the customer would feel receiving that product?"* These are essentially attempts to make offenders feel guilty about their actions, with the hope that they won't repeat them. But again, they could agree to your request but never consider the action wrong.

• **Don't appeal to physical consequences.** *"I'm giving you two days off without pay"* or *"You have to stay late or come in on the weekend and fix this."* These may be appropriate consequences, but consequences are not as effective—and are sometimes totally ineffective—when people do not believe in their heart they have done something wrong.

I have received a few speeding tickets in my 50+ years of driving, and they have become increasingly expensive. Today, a speeding ticket can cost several hundred dollars and may increase my insurance premiums. If I get too many tickets, my license can be suspended. In addition, people are more severely injured in high-speed wrecks. The consequences of speeding can be severe.

Yet, speeding is still a temptation. Why? Maybe I don't think I will get caught. Maybe I see others speeding and think that if they get away with it, so can I. Maybe I am in a hurry. Maybe I think I am a good driver and won't have a wreck. These may be good rationalizations, but the truth is, in my heart I don't really believe it is wrong to drive a few miles over the speed limit. If I truly believed it was wrong, I wouldn't do it.

Consequences alone are not always sufficient deterrents.

To change behavior, we need to agree about appropriate behavior and appeal to the conscience—not the mind, will, or emotions.

The following questions appeal to the conscience:

"Was that being truthful?"

"Were you punctual?"

"Were you exercising self-control?"

"Is speeding breaking the law?"

Reflect Grief

Reflecting grief is another way to help people realize how much their behavior has damaged our relationship. Grief is expressing anguish over the damage done to the relationship, whether it is a loss of trust, respect, or loyalty.

Some people have a problem conveying grief. There can be several reasons for this.

• **Lack of relationship.** If there is no relationship, there is nothing to grieve over because nothing is lost or broken.

• **Anger.** If you are angry, it is difficult to express grief. In addition, anger causes others to feel attacked and does not allow them to focus on the damaged relationship.

• **Lack of knowledge.** Not everyone knows how to express grief. Grief is a natural emotion we experience after a significant loss or great disappointment.

There are many ways to express grief, including silence, tears, facial expressions, and body language. When striving to help people understand the severity of their wrong actions, it is best to sit quietly, contemplate their actions, and think about how the relationship has been damaged. Punctuate the silence by asking a few questions that appeal to the conscience. Be prepared to invest time in this process. It may take an extended time of grieving before some people fully appreciate the damage inflicted by their behavior.

Never manipulate a person by feigning grief. If you are not grieving over the damaged relationship, you need to evaluate whether you are truly concerned about the success of the employee.

Look For Repentance—Not Regret

There is a saying: "You cannot repent without regret, but you can regret without repenting."

• *Regret* is sorrow about incurring the consequences of an action. It is associated with loss, not the wrongness of what was done. There is no change of heart associated with regret.

• *Repentance* literally means to turn and go the other direction. When people repent of an action, they change from believing the action was right to believing it was wrong. Repentance is followed by a desire to change.

One purpose of correction is to help people understand that what they did was wrong. You also want to inspire them to change. That is repentance.

Restore the Relationship

Repentance should be followed by a request for forgiveness. Unfortunately, many do not understand how to ask forgiveness or why it is important.

> *Forgiveness is not an emotion, forgiveness
> is an act of the will, and the will can
> function regardless of the temperature
> of the heart.* Corrie ten Boom

Many of us were taught as a child to say, "I'm sorry."

"I'm sorry" is not the same as asking forgiveness. "I'm sorry" accepts no responsibility for doing wrong. You can be "sorry" about the consequences without agreeing that what you did was wrong.

A true request for forgiveness includes an admission of what the offender did wrong. For example:

- "I was wrong for not being punctual. I know it causes a hardship on others. Will you forgive me?"
- "I was wrong when I failed to complete the work you assigned me. I will work to complete it, and I purpose to follow your instructions in the future. Will you forgive me?"

Many do not understand this, but as the leader you may need to take the initiative. Ask them, "Do you believe that what you did was wrong, and do you intend to change?" If you receive a positive response, you would answer, "I forgive you."

Asking for and receiving forgiveness clears the conscience and paves the way to restoring the relationship.

> *When a deep injury is done to us,*
> *we will never recover until we forgive.*
> Alan Stewart Paton

Administer Consequences

Repentance, forgiveness, and restoration do not necessarily remove consequences. Without repentance, even the most severe consequences may not bring about a change of heart. When there is true repentance, the consequences can be much more effective.

Consequences can be either *natural* or *structured*.

- We have a rule that prohibits employees from wearing gloves while operating a drill press. If an employee violated this rule, his glove might get caught in the drill, and his hand could be injured. That would be a natural consequence.
- A structured consequence is a predetermined correction for a specific behavior. If an employee was late to work and did not finish his work for the day, he might have to stay late to finish his tasks. That would be a structured consequence.

Leaders should determine what structured consequences will be given for wrong behavior. Our goal is to administer justice, and part of justice is administering the appropriate consequences. To be just, the consequences cannot be excessive.

Several years ago, people feared there would be a toilet-paper shortage. This sounds silly, but it caused a run on the stores, and toilet paper became scarce for a brief period. During that time, an employee was caught stealing toilet paper from Kimray. Our rules stated, "You will be fired for stealing." We felt that was too severe for stealing a roll of toilet paper, so we reduced the consequence and required the employee to replace what he took.

A previous policy at Kimray stated that if you quit, you were not eligible for rehiring. Several things happened that made us realize that was an unjust consequence. There are many reasons why someone may need to resign, and we had to re-evaluate our policy to make it more equitable. We revamped the rule, and now we have several leaders that worked for us, quit, and have returned. We would have missed having these high-quality leaders if the old policy was still in place.

Kimray provides random drug testing. A current policy at Kimray states that if you test positive, you lose your job. It is a valid, protective consequence. If you admit to a drug problem before a test, you are provided with drug rehabilitation. People who admit they have a problem and are seeking help should not be treated the same as people who are unwilling to accept responsibility for their actions.

The severity of the consequences should be structured to match, not exceed, the severity of the infraction. You do not want any punishments to be heavy-handed or excessive.

Evaluate the Results

Remember, the primary goal of correction is to restore a relationship. With that in mind, we need to evaluate the process. After every correction, you should take the time to gauge how you handled the situation. Here are a few questions to ask yourself after you are forced to issue correction:

- "Did I get angry?" Anger hinders the restoration process because the offender will react to your anger rather than focusing on the infraction.

- "Do I need to ask forgiveness? Did I do something wrong in the process? Did I confront the offender publicly or get angry?" If you did something wrong, be sure to clearly and humbly say, "I was wrong when I _____. Will you forgive me?"

- "Are the consequences just?" If not, change the consequences.

- "Which character qualities do I need to help this employee develop?"

- "Have I been consistent in my administration of rules and policies?"

- "Do we need to set new limitations?"

- "How can we help reinforce the decision this employee has made to change behavior?"

Wrap Up

You may be thinking, "Wow, this appears to be difficult." It is, and the first few times you correct an employee for character may be very difficult. But, as you practice and become familiar with the steps of correction, it will become easier. In addition, as you begin to reap the benefits of appropriate correction and restored relationships, you will become more confident about the process.

CHAPTER 19

GETTING STARTED

There is one thing that everyone who reads this book can start doing today—praising others for character. It requires no training. Simply use *definition, illustration,* and *benefit.* Review the chapter HOW TO PRAISE to hone your skills. Praising others for character costs you nothing, yet it is a simple and easy way to positively impact the lives of others every day.

Are you concerned that you won't remember the character qualities and their definitions? I can suggest three options to allow you to carry the list with you:

- You have permission to copy the character qualities and their definitions from *Appendix A* of this book.

- You can also access **www.characterfirst.com/download** to print the PDF document *Character Qualities & Definitions.*

- Also from **www.characterfirst.com**, you can click on Store to purchase a multifold, laminated *Pocket Guide* to carry in your pocket or purse for quick and easy reference to the character qualities and their definitions.

I carry a *Pocket Guide* with me most of the time and encourage you to do the same. Don't hesitate to pull it out and read a character quality and its definition when praising others.

Read through the list daily. You can review it anytime you have a few spare minutes, or make a habit of reviewing it at a specific time each day. Either way, you will quickly become familiar with the character qualities and the definitions. The more you praise and the more you use the character qualities and their definitions, the more proficient you will become.

What Is Next?

Have you made the decision that character is important? Do you understand that as a leader, you have an enormous impact on your employees? Do you desire to use your influence to inspire and guide them to success by building character?

I ask these questions because after 20 years of working with company leaders, I have observed that the key to successful implementation of Character First in any organization is the commitment of the leader. The success—*or failure*—of Character First ultimately lies with the leader. Character grows from the head down. It cannot be delegated or outsourced.

In addition, whenever you begin anything worthwhile, challenges will arise. If you are committed, you will face these challenges by asking, "What do we need to do to make this work?" If you are not fully committed when the challenges come, you will quit.

> *Never give in, never give in, never, never, never—in nothing, great or small, large or petty—never give in except to convictions of honor and good sense.* Winston Churchill

Still interested? The next step is to get a copy of this book for every leader in your organization and have them read it. Even if you don't adopt Character First, some may catch the vision and begin to praise others for character. Your organization will be better as a result and you may discover you have a *character champion.* In addition, your organization's leader should attend Character First training. If the leader cannot attend, then do what Frank Costa did: send a trusted manager whose advice and counsel will be followed. The training will be a hands-on, practical session on how to implement Character First in your organization. In addition, there will be opportunities to ask questions specific to your organization.

Set A Starting Date

Don't make the same mistake I made when we started at Kimray. Once you've participated in Character First training and decided to move forward, visit with your managers, cast the vision for character training, and set a starting date.

Be sure to allow time to adequately train all of your managers and give them the tools to be successful. Character First trainings are held at neutral locations where your managers can meet other managers, receive a comprehensive overview of Character First, practice praising for character, and be encouraged. They will benefit and become better managers as a result of attending the training.

Character First offers training in different locations in the United States or can provide training at your location. A list of trainings can be found at **www.characterfirst.com/events**. Contact Character First for information about on-site training.

Materials

An important part of the Character First initiative is providing the monthly Character First materials to employees. The materials explain the character quality of the month, provide discussion material for the Application Meetings, and give employees something to share with their family.

How Do You Measure Success?

A company's success is not defined by a higher profit margin, lower workers' compensation rates, higher productivity, lower turnover, or higher morale. These are the fruit produced by successful employees.

A company is successful when it changes lives, helps individuals build character, develops employees who are proud of where they work, and positively influences the community. Success is seeing employees work together in harmony, making wise decisions, being "others oriented," and demonstrating good character every day.

Individual success should not be measured by how much money you make, how big your house is, how many cars you own, what position you hold, or what title you have. Individual success is not determined by becoming famous or making a "notable" contribution to society. True success is making daily decisions based on good character. The vast majority of us will never be famous, but we can still have a positive impact on our family and the community. We can be known as men and women of character and integrity.

> *Fame is a vapor, popularity an accident,*
> *and riches take wing. Only one thing*
> *endures, and that is character.*
> Horace Greely

My grandfather was such a man. He was never famous, but he was known in the community as a man of character and integrity.

When I was about 12 years old, I had a thriving lawn-mowing business. I mowed several lawns a day all summer long, and my mower was worn out. Oil leaked around the crankshaft, fouled the spark plug, and made it difficult to start.

Each morning, the cowling and flywheel had to be removed and the spark plug cleaned. Then I could start the mower, but I had to push it from one lawn to another while it was running. I needed a new mower.

I didn't have enough money, so I went to the First National Bank of Pryor, Oklahoma. I walked up to the teller and told her I wanted to borrow $100 to buy a new mower. She smiled. Just then, a bank officer walked up and asked what I wanted. I repeated, "I want to borrow $100 to purchase a new lawn mower."

He responded, "Aren't you Wes Bavinger's grandson?"

I said, "Yes."

I will never forget his reply. "If you are Wes's grandson, you can have the loan," he said. "I know Wes, and he is good for it." As it turned out, I didn't have to borrow the money. My grandfather gave me his mower, and I repaid him by mowing his lawn each week.

What is the point of this story? Wes Bavinger was a man of character, and even if he wasn't famous, even if he didn't make any "notable" contribution to society, he made a lasting impact on me and on that community. When he looked you in the eye and gave you his word, you could count on it, and that meant something. His character influenced the community, and the town of Pryor was a better place because of him.

My hope is that you will apply Character First with the desire to create true success, and not just to improve the bottom line of your company. As McDonald's restaurant owner Reginald Jones said, "We do what's right because it's right to do what's right!" And the right thing to do is to help your employees be successful by strengthening their character.

The real "bottom line" is this. If you are committed to the principle that inspiring others to build character is the right thing to do, and if you have the determination to see it through, you will be successful.

> *Earn your success based on service*
> *to others, not at the expense of others.*
> H. Jackson Brown

Transformation

Most of this book is about how cultural transformation takes place when individuals within an organization are transformed—one by one. My experience, personally and with business leaders around the world, is that the most profound impact—*the greatest transformation*—takes place within the leader. Are you ready to improve your character? The challenge won't come from your employees. It won't come from your management team—or your family. The true challenge will come from within you.

As you praise people for character, lead employee meetings, talk about character, and give examples of character failures in your life, you will be challenged—sometimes many times a day. You can and will rise to this challenge, and you will come away transformed.

Will you join me in this adventure?

Your Character Determines Your Success

For additional information:
www.makingcharacterfirst.com
or
www.characterfirst.com

APPENDIX A

49 Character Qualities in Alphabetical Order

Alertness. Being aware of what is taking place around me so I can have the right responses.

Attentiveness. Showing the worth of a person or task by giving my undivided concentration.

Availability. Making my own schedule and priorities secondary to the wishes of those I serve.

Benevolence. Giving to others' basic needs without having as my motive personal reward.

Boldness. Confidence that what I have to say or do is true, right, and just.

Cautiousness. Knowing how important right timing is in accomplishing right actions.

Compassion. Investing whatever is necessary to heal the hurts of others.

Contentment. Realizing that true happiness does not depend on material conditions.

Creativity. Approaching a need, a task, or an idea from a new perspective.

Decisiveness. The ability to recognize key factors and finalize difficult decisions.

Deference. Limiting my freedom so I do not offend the tastes of those around me.

Dependability. Fulfilling what I consented to do, even if it means unexpected sacrifice.

Determination. Purposing to accomplish right goals at the right time, regardless of the opposition.

Diligence. Investing my time and energy to complete each task assigned to me.

Discernment. Understanding the deeper reasons why things happen.

Discretion. Recognizing and avoiding words, actions, and attitudes that could bring undesirable consequences.

Endurance. The inward strength to withstand stress and do my best.

Enthusiasm. Expressing joy in each task as I give it my best effort.

Faith. Confidence that actions rooted in good character will yield the best outcome, even when I cannot see how.

Flexibility. Willingness to change plans or ideas without getting upset.

Forgiveness. Clearing the record of those who have wronged me and not holding a grudge.

Generosity. Carefully managing my resources so I can freely give to those in need.

Gentleness. Showing consideration and personal concern for others.

Gratefulness. Letting others know by my words and actions how they have benefited my life.

Honor. Respecting others because of their worth as human beings.

Hospitality. Cheerfully sharing food, shelter, or conversation to benefit others.

Humility. Acknowledging that achievement results from the investment of others in my life.

Initiative. Recognizing and doing what needs to be done before I am asked to do it.

Joyfulness. Maintaining a good attitude, even when faced with unpleasant conditions.

Justice. Taking personal responsibility to uphold what is pure, right, and true.

Loyalty. Using difficult times to demonstrate my commitment to those I serve.

Meekness. Yielding my personal rights and expectations with a desire to serve.

Obedience. Quickly and cheerfully carrying out the direction of those who are responsible for me.

Orderliness. Arranging myself and my surroundings to achieve greater efficiency.

Patience. Accepting a difficult situation without giving a deadline to remove it.

Persuasiveness. Guiding vital truths around another's mental roadblocks.

Punctuality. Showing esteem for others by doing the right thing at the right time.

Resourcefulness. Finding practical uses for that which others would overlook or discard.

Responsibility. Knowing and doing what is expected of me.

Security. Structuring my life around that which cannot be destroyed or taken away.

Self-Control. Rejecting wrong desires and doing what is right.

Sensitivity. Perceiving the true attitudes and emotions of those around me.

Sincerity. Eagerness to do what is right with transparent motives.

Thoroughness. Knowing what factors will diminish the effectiveness of my work or words if neglected.

Thriftiness. Allowing myself and others to spend only what is necessary.

Tolerance. Realizing that everyone is at varying levels of character development.

Truthfulness. Earning future trust by accurately reporting past facts.

Virtue. The moral excellence evident in my life as I consistently do what is right.

Wisdom. Seeing and responding to life situations from a perspective that transcends my current circumstances.

Permission granted to reproduce definitions for personal or educational use. Download the definitions at www.characterfirst.com/downloads

APPENDIX B

Sample Interview Questions

Punctuality:
Would your previous supervisors say that you are consistently on time? _____
Why or why not? _____

Would your previous employers say that your attendance was:
Excellent _____ Good _____ Fair _____ Poor _____
Please explain. _____

Orderliness:
Would your past supervisors say you are orderly?
Yes _____ No _____
What does "being orderly" mean to you?

Truthfulness:
Would those that know you best say that your word can be trusted? Yes _____ No _____
Why or why not? _____

Dependability:
Have you ever had to experience loss for doing what is right?
Yes _____ No _____
Please explain. _____

Loyalty and Contentment:
Was the previous company you worked for a good company?
Yes _____ No _____
Please explain. _____

Was your previous employer fair with regards to pay?
Yes _____ No _____
Please explain. _____

Obedience:

Would your previous supervisor say you were good at following instructions? Yes _____ No _____

Why or why not? _____

Please give an example. _____

Forgiveness and Tolerance:

Would your past supervisors say you get angry:

Never _____ Rarely _____ Sometimes _____ Often _____

What causes you to get upset on the job? _____

Have you ever asked a co-worker or supervisor for forgiveness for doing wrong? Yes _____ No _____

Please explain. _____

Please check the areas in which you are weakest:

___ Contentment	___ Diligence	___ Dependability
___ Integrity	___ Loyalty	___ Meekness
___ Forgiveness	___ Orderliness	___ Punctuality
___ Truthfulness	___ Obedience	___ Self-control

Please check the areas in which you are the strongest:

___ Contentment	___ Diligence	___ Dependability
___ Integrity	___ Loyalty	___ Meekness
___ Forgiveness	___ Orderliness	___ Punctuality
___ Truthfulness	___ Obedience	___ Self-control

What are your goals? _____

How will this job help you achieve your goals? _____

_____

Why do you want to work for this company? _____

_____

APPENDIX C

Signs of Anger

"raises his voice"

"yells"

"criticizes"

"is really quiet"

"He gets quiet & distant."

"Sighs"

"Complains about how the house looks."

"He puts up a wall."

"My husband says very hurtful things (hurts to the bone)."

"voice—in answering louder & short"

"He sighs, becomes withdrawn, sometimes gives the silent treatment."

"looks down & doesn't talk"

"facial expression"

"gruff voice"

"Short, abrupt, jerky movements (resulting most times in broken things)

"humiliates"

"no patience with children"

"takes matters into his own hands"

"crosses arms & leans back with right foot extended outward by about 6 or more inches – he does this while either sitting or standing" "face becomes stern"

"Is impatient with me and the children"

"non-smiling"

"His brow creases."

"body tenseness"

"silence, won't express what is wrong"

"cussing"

"Silence—can be for hours"

"Argues in response to everything I say."

"Becomes aggressive."

"dark eyes"

"He busies himself by cleaning the house and working in the yard."

"abrupt"

"shuts us out or ignores us."

"Doesn't want to talk about it."

"Snaps at children and I."

"Distant"

"He won't listen"

"stiff neck, body"

"He becomes resistant"

"Unapproachable"

"Cold—cannot get close, lack of response when hugged"

"Really, he is so angry that all he has to do is walk in a room & we feel his anger. We are always 'walking on eggshells.'"

APPENDIX D

List of Quotes

A tree is known by its fruit; A man by his deeds. **Saint Basil**

Of all the properties which belong to honorable men, not one is so highly prized as that of character. **Henry Clay**

Reputation is what men and women think of us; character is what God and the angels know of us. **Thomas Paine**

A man's character is his fate. **Heraclitus**

Character may be manifested in the great moments, but it is made in the small ones. **Phillip Brooks**

The measure of a man's character is what he would do it he knew he would never be found out.
Baron Thomas Babington Macauley

Good character dictates right attitudes, right words, and right actions, not just when it is easy but in very difficult situations. **Character First**

He who walks with the wise grows wise, but a companion of fools suffers harm. **Proverbs 13:20**

Associate yourself with men of good quality if you esteem your own reputation; for 'tis better to be alone than in bad company. **George Washington**

Character is the by-product; it is produced in the great man-ufacture of daily duty. **Woodrow T. Wilson**

We imagine we would be all right if a big crisis arose, but the crisis will only reveal the stuff we are made of. It will not put anything into us… Crisis always reveals character.
Oswald Chambers

Sow a thought, and you reap an act;
Sow an act, and you reap a habit;
Sow a habit, and you reap a character;
Sow a character, and you reap a destiny.
Unknown

Character consists of what you do on the third and fourth try.
James A. Michener

Character is much easier kept than recovered.
Thomas Paine

If you feel constrained to look for mistakes, use a mirror not a telescope. **Unknown**

Don't wait until people do things exactly right before you praise them. **Ken Blanchard**

A child is molded by the praise of his parents.
A man is molded by the praise of his wife.
An employee is molded by the praise of his boss.
Character First

In school—you get what you test.
At work—you get what you require.
With people—you get what you praise. **Character First**

Be just as enthusiastic about the success of others as you are about your own. **Christian Larson**

I am what I am today because of the choices I made yesterday. **Unknown**

Character is like a tree and reputation like its shadow.
The shadow is what we think of it; the tree is the real thing.
Thomas Paine

Successful individuals make successful families.
Successful families make successful organizations.
Successful individuals, families, and organizations make successful cities, states, and countries.
Character determines success. **Character First**

The fastest way to drive an employee insane is to give him or her new responsibilities and fail to provide the necessary instruction and training to do the job. **Ken Blanchard**

Each person has his own strong points. **Aesop**

Character determines success. **Character First**

A man's treatment of money is the most decisive test of his character, how he makes it and how he spends it.
James Moffat

Your best résumé is not what you write, but how you live.
Unknown

I have never been hurt by something I didn't say.
Calvin Coolidge

Example isn't another way to teach, it is the only way to teach. **Albert Einstein**

Sharing your successes builds walls.
Sharing your failures builds bridges. **Tom Hill**

Character First can change our schools.
It can change our homes.
It can change our businesses.
Character First can change our world. **Tom Hill**

I have but one lamp by which my feet are guided, and that is the lamp of experience. I know no other way of judging the future but by the past. **Patrick Henry**

Hire for character—train for skills. **Character First**

Men are respectable only as they respect. **Emerson**

Speak when you are angry and you'll make the best speech you'll ever regret. **Lawrence J. Peter**

Your walk walks and your talk talks,
but your walk talks louder than your talk talks. **Anonymous**

It takes a great man to make a good listener. **Arthur Helps**

Men count up the faults of those that keep them waiting.
French Proverb

He who is slow to anger is better than the mighty; and he who rules his spirit better than he who captures a walled city.
Proverbs 16:32

Keep your temper, nobody else wants it. **Unknown**

Forgiveness is not an emotion, forgiveness is an act of the will, and the will can function regardless of the temperature of the heart. **Corrie ten Boom**

When a deep injury is done to us, we will never recover until we forgive. **Alan Stewart Paton**

Never give in, never give in, never, never, never—in nothing, great or small, large or petty—never give in except to convictions of honor and good sense. **Winston Churchill**

Fame is a vapor, popularity an accident, riches take wing, and only character endures. **Horace Greely**

Earn your success based on service to others, not at the expense of others. **H. Jackson Brown**

NOTES

1. "Focus on Character Reaps Big Savings, Reductions of Comp Costs and Claims," *Bureau of National Affairs' Workers' Compensation Report 7*, no. 9 (1996): 217-18.

2. Hilb Rogel and Hamilton Company of Oklahoma to Kimray Inc., August 26, 1994, in author Tom Hill's possession.

3. "Tips to Control Workers' Compensation Costs," in author Tom Hill's possession.

4. "Control Insurance Costs: Manage Your Risks," in author Tom Hill's possession.

5. Richard L. Hughes, Robert C. Ginnett and Gordon J. Curphy, *Leadership: Enhancing the Lessons of Experience,* (New York: Irwin/McGraw Hill, 2008), 412; Pace Communications, Inc., *Hemispheres Magazine*, November 1994, 155; "Keeping Workers Happy," *USA Today*, February 10, 1998.

6. Ken Blanchard and Spencer Johnson, *The One Minute Manager* (New York: William Morrow and Company, Inc. 1982), 61.

7. "Words of Praise From a PC," *Communications Briefings* 18, no. 4 (1999).

8. Marilyn Gardner, "Seven things employees want most to be happy at work," *The Christian Science Monitor*, January 28, 2008.

9. Cliff Uranga and Argyl Dick, "Chaplaincy Group Teams With Detention to Address Spiritual Needs and Character," *LJN Exchange* (2005): 25-28.

10. Bill Sherman, "Faith Builds Character," *Tulsa World*, December 18, 2008.

11. Ibid.

12. Des Tobin, Frank Costa: *Faith, Family and Footy* (Malvern: Killaghy Publishing, 2007), 101-02.

13. Jim Collins, *Good To Great* (New York: Harper Business, 2001), 41.

14. American Council for Drug Education's Facts for Employers, "Why Worry About Drugs and Alcohol in the Workplace?" http://www.acde.org/employer/DAwork.htm.

15. Jim Collins, *Good To Great* (New York: Harper Business, 2001), 51.

16. "Workplace Killers", *USA Today*, Sept. 28, 1999.

17. D.T. Phillips, "The Price Tag of Turnover," *Personnel Journal* 69, no. 12 (1990): 58.

18. Kenneth Thomas and Warren Schmidt, "A Survey of Managerial Interests With Respect to Conflict," *The Academy of Management Journal* 19, no. 2 (1976): 315-18.

19. Carol Watson and L. Richard Hoffman, "Managers as Negotiators," *The Leadership Quarterly* 7, no. 1 (1996): 63-85.

20. John Maxwell, "People Do What People See," *Bloomberg Businessweek*, November 19, 2007.

What is Character First?

Character First is a leadership development program based on character that is delivered many ways— training seminars, books, magazines, curriculum, email— that focus on real-life issues at work, school, home, and the community.

Our monthly magazine goes to 40,000 business subscribers throughout the United States, and our K-12 school curriculum is taught in more than 20 countries.

Who uses Character First?

- Fortune 1000 Companies
- Small & Medium Enterprises
- Government Agencies & Non-Profits
- Public & Private Schools
- Families

Contact:

Call 877-357-0001 or visit **www.characterfirst.com** to learn how Character First can benefit you and your organization!